King of Great Britain

New commission of the governor of Quebec and other instruments of authority derived from the crown relative to America

King of Great Britain

New commission of the governor of Quebec and other instruments of authority derived from the crown relative to America

ISBN/EAN: 9783337274351

Printed in Europe, USA, Canada, Australia, Japan

Cover: Foto ©Suzi / pixelio.de

NEW COMMISSION

OF THE

GOVERNOR

OF

QUEBEC;

AND OTHER

INSTRUMENTS

OF

AUTHORITY,

DERIVED FROM THE

CROWN

RELATIVE TO

AMERICA.

The New Commiſſion of the Governor of the Province of QUEBECK.

GEORGE the THIRD, by the Grace of God, of Great Britain, France, and Ireland, King, Defender of the Faith, &c. To our truſty and well-beloved Guy Carleton, *Eſquire, greeting.*

WHEREAS we did by our letters patent under our great ſeal of Great Britain, bearing date at Weſtminſter the twelfth day of April, in the eighth year of our reign, conſtitute and appoint you to be our captain general and governor in chief in and over our province of Quebec in America, bounded on the Labrador coaſt by the river St. John, and from thence by a line drawn from the head of that river through the lake St. John to the ſouth-eaſt of lake Nipiſſin, from whence the ſaid line, croſſing the river St. Lawrence and lake Champlain in forty-five degrees of northern latitude, paſſes along the high lands, which divide the rivers that empty themſelves into the ſaid river St. Lawrence, from thoſe which fall into the ſea, and alſo along the north coaſt of the bay *des Chaleurs*, and the coaſt of the gulph of St. Lawrence to cape Rozieres, and from thence croſſing the mouth of the river St. Lawrence by the weſt end of the iſland of Anticoſti, terminates at the aforeſaid river St. John, together with all the rights, members, and appurtenances whatſoever thereunto belonging, for and during our will and pleaſure, as by the ſaid recited letters patent, relation being thereunto had, may more fully and at large appear. And whereas we did alſo by our letters patent under our great ſeal of Great Britain, bearing date at Weſtminſter, the day of in the year of our reign, conſtitute and appoint Molineux Shuldham, eſq. to be our governor and commander in chief in and over our island of Newfoundland, and all the coast of Labrador, from the entrance of Hudson's streights to the river St. John, which discharges itself into the sea nearly opposite the west end of the island of Anticosti, including that island, with any other small islands on the said coast of Labrador, and also the islands of Madelaine in the gulph of St. Lawrence, as also of all our forts and garrisons erected and established in our said islands of Newfoundland, Anticosti, and Madelaine, or on the coast of Labrador within the limits aforesaid, for and during our will and pleasure, as by the said letters patent, relation being thereunto had, may more fully and at large appear.

Revocation of the last patent.

Now know you, that we have revoked and determined, and by these presents revoke and determine, the said recited letters patent granted to you, the said Guy Carleton, as aforesaid, and every clause, article, and thing therein contained; and that we have also revoked and determined, and do by these presents revoke and determine so much and such part of the said recited letters patent granted to Molineux Shuldham, esq. as aforesaid, as relates to the coast of Labrador, including the island of Anticosti, with any other small islands on the said coast of Labrador, and every clause, article, and thing therein contained, so far as the same relates to the said coast of Labrador, and the islands herein before recited.

Commission to be capt. gen. and gov. in chief of the province.

And further know you, that we reposing especial trust and confidence in the prudence, courage, and loyalty of you, the said Guy Carleton, of our especial grace, certain knowledge, and mere motion, have thought fit to constitute and appoint you, the said Guy Carleton, to be our captain-general and governor in chief in and over our province of Quebeck in America, comprehending all our territories, islands, and countries in North America, bounded on the

Boundaries of the province.

south by a line from the bay of Chaleurs along the high lands, which divide the rivers that empty themselves into the river St. Lawrence, from those which fall into the sea, to a point in forty-five degrees of northern latitude, on the eastern bank of the river Connecticut; keeping the same latitude directly west through the lake Champlain, until in the same latitude it meets with the river St. Lawrence, from thence up the eastern bank of the said river to the lake Ontario, thence through the lake Ontario, and the river, commonly called Niagara, and thence along by the eastern and south eastern bank of lake Erie, following the said bank, until the same shall be intersected fected by the northern boundary granted by the charter of the province of Penſylvania, in caſe the ſame ſhall be ſo interſected, and from thence along the ſaid northern and weſtern boundaries of the ſaid province, until the ſaid weſtern boundary ſtrikes the Ohio; but, in caſe the ſaid bank of the ſaid lake ſhall not be found to be ſo interſected, then following the ſaid bank, until it ſhall arrive at the point of the ſaid bank, which ſhall be neareſt to the north-weſtern angle of the ſaid province of Penſylvania, and thence by a right line to the ſaid north-weſtern angle of the ſaid province, and thence along the weſtern boundary of the ſaid province, until it ſtrikes the river Ohio, and along the bank of the ſaid river weſtward to the banks of Miſſiſſippi, and northward along the eaſtern bank of the ſaid river to the ſouthern boundary of the territory granted to the merchants adventurers of England trading to Hudſon's Bay; and alſo all ſuch territories, iſlands, and countries, which have, ſince the tenth of February, 1763, been made part of the government of Newfoundland, as aforeſaid, together with all the rights, members, and appurtenances whatſoever thereunto belonging.

Gov. to act according to the powers and directions of this commiſſion, and according to the King's inſtructions.

And we do hereby require and command you to do and execute all things in due manner, that ſhall belong to your ſaid command, and the truſt we have repoſed in you, according to the ſeveral powers and directions granted or appointed you by this preſent commiſſion, and the inſtructions and authorities herewith given unto you, or by ſuch further powers, inſtructions, and authorities as ſhall at any time hereafter be granted or appointed you under our ſignet or ſign manual, or by our order in our privy council, and according to ſuch ordinances as ſhall hereafter be made and agreed upon by you, with the advice and conſent of the council of our ſaid province under your government, in ſuch manner and form as is herein after expreſſed.

Oaths to be taken by the gov.

And our will and pleaſure is, that you, the ſaid Guy Carleton, do, after the publication of theſe our letters patent, in ſuch manner and form as has been accuſtomed to be uſed on like occaſions, in the firſt place take the oaths appointed to be taken by an act paſſed in the firſt year of the reign of King George the Firſt, intituled, "*An act for the further ſecurity of his Majeſty's perſon and government, and the ſucceſſion of the crown in the heirs of the late princeſs Sophia, being proteſtants, and for extinguiſhing the hopes of the pretended prince of Wales, and his open and ſecret abettors*; and by an act paſſed in

Thoſe appointed by 1 Geo. I.

Thoſe appointed by 6 Geo. III.

in the ſixth year of our reign, intituled, "*An act for altering the oath of abjuration, and the aſſurance; and for amending ſo much of an act of the ſeventh year of her late majeſty Queen Anne, intituled, An act for the improvement of the union of the two kingdoms, as, after the time therein limitted, requires the delivery of certain liſts and copies therein mentioned, to perſons indicted of high treaſon, or miſpriſion of treaſon;*" as alſo that you make and ſubſcribe the declaration mentioned in an act of parliament, made in the twenty-fifth year of the reign of King Charles the Second, intituled, "*An act for preventing dangers which may happen from Popiſh recuſants;*" and likewiſe that you take the oath uſually taken by the governors in the plantations, for the due execution of the office and truſt of our captain-general and governor in and over our ſaid province, and for the due and impartial adminiſtration of juſtice; and further that you take the oath required to be taken by governors of the plantations, to do their utmoſt, that the ſeveral laws relating to trade and the plantations be duly obſerved; which ſaid oaths and declaration our council of our ſaid province, or any three of the members thereof, have hereby full power and authority, and are required to tender and adminiſter to you; all which being duly performed, you ſhall yourſelf adminiſter to each of the members of our ſaid council, (except as herein after excepted) the ſaid oaths mentioned in the ſaid acts, intituled, "*An act for the further ſecurity of his Majeſty's perſon and government, and the ſucceſſion of the crown in the heirs of the late princeſs Sophia, being proteſtants, and for extinguiſhing the hopes of the pretended prince of Wales, and his open and ſecret abettors;*" and "*An act for altering the oath of abjuration, and the aſſurance, and for amending ſo much of an act of the ſeventh year of her late majeſty Queen Anne, intituled, An act for the improvement of the union of the two kingdoms, as after the time therein limitted, requires the delivery of certain liſts and copies, therein mentioned, to perſons indicted of high treaſon, or miſpriſion of treaſon;*" as alſo cauſe them to make and ſubſcribe the aforementioned declaration, and to adminiſter unto them the uſual oath for the due execution of their places and truſts.

Declaration againſt tranſubſtantion, 25 Car. II. Oath of office, and oath concerning the law of trade.

Oaths to be taken by members of the council.

Thoſe of the romiſh religion, exempt from all oaths;

And whereas we may find it expedient for our ſervice, that our council of our ſaid province ſhould be in part compoſed of ſuch of our Canadian ſubjects, or their deſcendants, as remain within the ſame under the faith of the treaty of Paris, and who may profeſs the religion of the church of Rome; it is therefore our will and pleaſure, that in all caſes

where

where ſuch perſons ſhall or may be admitted, either into our ſaid council or into any other offices, they ſhall be exempted from all teſts, and from taking any other oath than that preſcribed in and by an act of parliament, paſſed in the fourteenth year of our reign, intituled, "*An act for making more effectual proviſion for the government of the province of Quebeck in North America*; and alſo the uſual oath for the due execution of their places and truſts reſpectively.

except that preſcribed by ſtat. 14 Geo. III.

And we do further give and grant unto you, the ſaid Guy Carleton, full power and authority from time to time, and at any time hereafter, by yourſelf, or by any other to be authorized by you in that behalf, to adminiſter and give the oaths mentioned in the ſaid acts, intituled, "*An act for the further ſecurity of his Majeſty's perſon and government, and the ſucceſſion of the crown in the heirs of the late princeſs Sophia, being proteſtants, and for extinguiſhing the hopes of the pretended prince of Wales, and his open and ſecret abettors*," and, "*An act for altering the oath of abjuration, and the aſſurance; and for amending ſo much of an act of the ſeventh year of her late majeſty Queen Anne, intituled, An act for the improvement of the union of the two kingdoms, as, after the time therein limitted, requires the delivery of certain liſts and copies therein mentioned, to perſons indicted of high treaſon, or miſpriſion of treaſon*," to all and every ſuch perſon or perſons, as you ſhall think fit, who ſhall at any time or times paſs into our ſaid province, or ſhall be reſident or abiding there.

Power for the governor to adminiſter or impower others to adminiſter the ſaid oaths.

And we do hereby authorize and impower you to keep and uſe the public ſeal of our province of Quebeck for ſealing all things whatſoever, that ſhall paſs the great ſeal of our ſaid province.

Power to uſe public ſeal.

And we do hereby give and grant unto you, the ſaid Guy Carleton, full power and authority, with the advice and conſent of our ſaid council, to make ordinances for the peace, welfare, and good government of the ſaid province, and of the people and inhabitants thereof, and ſuch others, as ſhall reſort thereunto, and for the benefit of us, our heirs, and ſucceſſors; provided always, that nothing herein contained ſhall extend, or be conſtrued to extend to the authoriſing and impowering the paſſing any ordinance or ordinances for laying any taxes or duties within the ſaid province, ſuch rates and taxes only excepted, as the inhabitants of any town or diſtrict within our ſaid province may be authorized

Power with conſent of the council to make ordinances;

thorized by any ordinance passed by you, with the advice and consent of the said council, to assess, levy, and apply within the said town or district for the purpose of making roads, erecting and repairing public buildings, or for any other purpose respecting the local convenience and œconomy of such town or district; provided also, that every ordinance, so to be made by you, by and with the advice and consent of the said council, shall be, within six months from the passing thereof, transmitted to us under our seal of our said province for our approbation or disallowance of the same; as also duplicates thereof by the next conveyance; and in case any, or all of the said ordinances shall at any time be disallowed and not approved, and so signified by us, our heirs and successors by order in their, or our privy council unto you, the said Guy Carleton, or to the commander in chief of our said province for the time being, then such and so many of the said ordinances, as shall be so disallowed and not approved, shall from the promulgation of the said order in council within the said province cease, determine and become utterly void and of no effect; provided also, that no ordinance touching religion, or by which any punishment may be inflicted greater than fine or imprisonment for three months, shall be of any force or effect, until the same shall have been allowed and confirmed by us, our heirs and successors, and such allowance or confirmation signified to you, or to the commander in chief of our said province for the time being, by their or our order in their or our privy council.

which shall be transmitted to England within six months;

Provided also, that no ordinance shall be passed at any meeting of the council, where less than a majority of the whole council is present, or at any time, except between the first day of January and the first day of May, unless upon some urgent occasion; in which case every member thereof resident at the town of Quebeck, or within fifty miles thereof, shall be personally summoned to attend the same: and to the end that nothing may be passed or done by our said council to the prejudice of us, our heirs, and successors, we will and ordain, that you, the said Guy Carleton, shall have and enjoy a negative voice in the making and passing of all ordinances, as aforesaid.

But none to pass unless a majority of the council be present, or between Jan. 1, and May 1.

Govern. to have a negative voice.

And we do by these presents give and grant unto you, the said Guy Carleton, full power and authority, with the advice and consent of our said council, to erect, constitute, and establish such and so many courts of judicature and public

Power with consent of the council to erect courts of judicature;

public justice within our said province under your government, as you and they shall think fit and necessary for the hearing and determining all causes, as well criminal as civil, and for awarding execution thereupon, with all reasonable and necessary powers, authorities, fees, and privileges belonging thereunto; as also to appoint and commissionate fit persons in the several parts of your government to administer the oaths mentioned in the aforesaid acts, intituled, "*An act for the further security of his Majesty's person and government; and the succession of the crown in the heirs of the late princess Sophia, being protestants; and for extinguishing the hopes of the pretended prince of Wales, and his open and secret abettors;*" and, "*An act for altering the oath of abjuration, and the assurance; and for amending so much of an act of the seventh year of her late majesty queen Anne, intituled, An act for the improvement of the union of the two kingdoms, as, after the time therein limitted, requires the delivery of certain lists and copies, therein mentioned, to persons indicted of high treason, or misprision of treason;*" as also to tender and administer the aforesaid declaration to such persons belonging to the said courts, as shall be obliged to take the same.

and to commissionate fit persons to administer the aforesaid oaths to persons belonging to such courts.

And we do hereby grant unto you full power and authority to constitute and appoint judges, and in cases requisite commissioners of Oyer and Terminer, justices of the peace, sheriffs, and other necessary officers and ministers in our said province for the better administration of justice, and putting the laws in execution; and to administer or cause to be administered unto them such oath or oaths, as are usually given for the due execution and performance of offices and places, and for the clearing of truth in judicial causes.

Power to appoint judges, commissioners of Oyer and Terminer, justices of the peace, and other officers of justice.

And we do hereby give and grant unto you full power and authority, where you shall see cause, or shall judge any offender or offenders in criminal matters, or for any fines or forfeitures due unto us, fit objects of our mercy, to pardon all such offenders, and remit all such offences, fines, and forfeitures; treason and wilful murder only excepted; in which cases you shall likewise have power upon extraordinary occasions to grant reprieves to the offenders, until, and to the intent our royal pleasure may be known therein.

Power to pardon crimes.

And we do by these presents give and grant unto you full power and authority to collate any person or persons to any churches,

Power to collate to ecclesiastical benefices.

churches, chapels, or other ecclesiastical benefices within our said province, as often as any of them shall happen to be void.

Power to levy troops and employ them against enemies, pirates, and rebels;

And we do hereby give and grant unto you, the said Guy Carleton, by yourself, or by your captains and commanders by you to be authorized, full power and authority to levy, arm, muster, command, and employ all persons whatsoever residing within our said province; and, as occasion shall serve, them to march, embark, or transport from one place to another, for the resisting and withstanding of all enemies, pirates, and rebels both at land and sea; and to transport such forces to any of our plantations in America, if necessity shall require, for defence of the same against the invasion or attempts of any of our enemies; and such enemies, pirates and rebels, if there shall be occasion, to pursue and prosecute in, or out of, the limits of our said province; and, if it shall so please God, them to vanquish, apprehend, and take, and, being taken, according to law to put to death, or keep or preserve alive at your discretion, and to execute martial law in time of invasion, war, or other times, when by law it may be executed; and to do and execute all and every other thing and things, which to our captain-general and governor in chief doth or of right ought to belong.

and to execute martial law, in time of war.

Power with consent of the council, to build forts and castles;

And we do hereby give and grant unto you full power and authority, by and with the advice and consent of our said council, to erect, raise, and build in our said province such and so many forts, platforms, castles, cities, boroughs, towns, and fortifications, as you by the advice aforesaid shall judge necessary; and the same or any of them to fortify and furnish with ordnance, ammunition, and all sorts of arms fit and necessary for the security and defence of our said province; and, by the advice aforesaid, the same again, or any of them to demolish or dismantle, as may be most convenient.

and to fortify and furnish them with arms, &c. and to demolish or dismantle them.

Power to appoint captains and other officers of ships, and to grant them commissions to execute the law martial.

And forasmuch as divers mutinies and disorders may happen by persons shipped and employed at sea, during the time of war; and to the end, that such, as shall be shipped and employed at sea during the time of war, may be better governed and ordered, we do hereby give and grant unto you, the said Guy Carleton, full power and authority to constitute and appoint captains, lieutenants, masters of ships, and other commanders and officers; and to grant to such captains, lieutenants, masters of ships, and other com-

manders

manders and officers, commiſſions to execute the law martial during the time of war, according to the directions of an act paſſed in the twenty-ſecond year of the reign of our late royal grandfather, intituled, "*An act for amending, explaining, and reducing into one act of parliament, the laws relating to the government of his Majeſty's ſhips, veſſels, and forces by ſea;*" and to uſe ſuch proceedings, authorities, puniſhments, corrections, and executions upon any offender or offenders, who ſhall be mutinous, ſeditious, diſorderly, or any way unruly either at ſea, or during the time of their abode or reſidence in any of the ports, harbours, or bays in our ſaid province, as the caſe ſhall be found to require, according to martial law; and the ſaid directions, during the the time of war, as aforeſaid.

Provided, that nothing herein contained ſhall be conſtrued to the enabling you, or any by your authority to hold plea, or have any juriſdiction of any offence, cauſe, matter, or thing committed or done upon the high ſea, or within any of the havens, rivers, or creeks of our ſaid province under your government, by any captain, commander, lieutenant, maſter, officer, ſeaman, ſoldier, or perſon whatſoever, who ſhall be in actual ſervice and pay, in or on board any of our ſhips of war, or other veſſels acting by immediate commiſſion or warrant from our commiſſioners for executing the office of our high admiral of Great Britain, or from our high admiral of Great Britain for the time being, under the ſeal of our admiralty; but that ſuch captain, commander, lieutenant, maſter, officer, ſeaman, ſoldier, or other perſon ſo offending, ſhall be left to be proceeded againſt, and tried, as their offences ſhall require, either by commiſſion under our great ſeal of this kingdom, as the ſtatute of the twenty-eighth of Henry VIII. directs; or by commiſſion from our ſaid commiſſioners for executing the office of high admiral of Great Britain, or from our high admiral of Great Britain for the time being, according to the aforementioned act, intituled, "*An act for amending, explaining, and reducing into one act of parliament, the laws relating to the government of his Majeſty's ſhips, veſſels, and forces by ſea*; and not otherwiſe.

This ſhall not affect any officers, &c. on board ſhips commiſſioned by the admiralty, when they commit offences either on the high ſea, or in any river, creek, or haven. But theſe perſons ſhall be tried for ſuch offences either by commiſſions under the great ſeal of Great Britain or by commiſſion from the admiralty.

Provided nevertheleſs, that all diſorders and miſdemeanors committed on ſhore by any captain, commander, lieutenant, maſter, officer, ſeaman, ſoldier, or other perſon whatſoever belonging to any of our ſhips of war, or other veſſels acting by

But for offences committed on ſhore, thoſe perſons ſhall be tried and punished according to the laws of the place where the offence shall be committed.

by immediate commission or warrant from our commissioners for executing the office of high admiral of Great Britain, or from our high admiral of Great Britain for the time being, under the seal of our admiralty, may be tried and punished according to the laws of the place, where any such disorders, offences, and misdemeanors shall be committed on shore; notwithstanding such offender be in our actual service, and borne in our pay on board any such our ships of war, or other vessels acting by immediate commission, or warrant from our commissioners for executing the office of high admiral of Great Britain, or from our high admiral of Great Britain for the time being, as aforesaid, so as he shall not receive any protection for the avoiding of justice for such offences committed on shore from any pretence of his being employed in our service at sea.

Power with consent of the council to dispose of public monies, for support of government

And our further will and pleasure is, that all public monies granted and raised for the public uses of our said province, be issued out by warrant from you, by and with the advice and consent of our council, as aforesaid, for the support of the government, and not otherwise.

Power with consent of the council, to grant lands.

And we likewise give and grant unto you full power and authority, by and with the advice and consent of our said council, to settle and agree with the inhabitants of our said province for such lands, tenements, and hereditaments, as now are, or hereafter shall be in our power to dispose of, and them to grant to any person or persons upon such terms and under such moderate quit-rents, services, and acknowledgements to be thereupon reserved unto us, as you, with the advice aforesaid, shall think fit; which said grants are to pass, and be sealed by our public seal of our said province, and being entered upon record by such officer or officers as shall be appointed thereunto, shall be good and effectual in law against us, our heirs and successors.

Grants to be under the public seal and to be registered.

Power, with consent of the council to appoint fairs, &c.

And we do hereby give you the said Guy Carleton full power and authority to order and appoint fairs, marts, and markets; as also such and so many ports, harbours, bays, havens, and other places for the conveniency and security of shipping, and for the better loading and unloading of goods and merchandizes, in such and so many places, as by you, with the advice and consent of our said council, shall be thought fit and necessary.

All officers, &c. to aid and assist the

And we do hereby require and command all officers and ministers, civil and military, and all other inhabitants of our

our said province to be obedient, aiding, and assisting unto you, the said Guy Carleton, in the execution of this our commission, and of the powers and authorities therein contained; and in case of your death or absence from our said province and government, to be obedient, aiding, and assisting, as aforesaid, to the lieutenant governor or commander in chief for the time being, to whom we do therefore by these presents give and grant all and singular the powers and authorities herein granted to be by him executed and enjoyed, during our pleasure, or until your arrival within our said province.

governor in the execution of his commission.

And if upon your death or absence out of our said province, there be no person upon the place commissionated or appointed by us to be lieutenant governor or commander in chief of our said province; our will and pleasure is, that the eldest councillor, being a natural born subject of Great Britain, Ireland, or the plantations, and professing the protestant religion, who shall be at the time of your death or absence residing within our said province, shall take upon him the administration of the government, and execute our said commission and instructions, and the several powers and authorities therein contained, in the same manner and to all intents and purposes, as other our governor or commander in chief should or ought to do, in case of your absence, until your return, and in all cases until our further pleasure be known therein.

who to be commander in chief of the province, in case of the death or absence of the governor.

And we do hereby declare, ordain, and appoint, that you, the said Guy Carleton, shall and may hold, execute, and enjoy the office and place of our captain general and governor in chief, in and over our said province of Quebeck, and all the territories dependent thereon; with all and singular the powers and authorities hereby granted unto you, for and during our will and pleasure.

This office to be held during the King's pleasure.

In witness whereof we have caused these our letters to be made patent; witness ourself at Westminster, the day of in the year of our reign.

Former

Former COMMISSION of CAPTAIN GENERAL and GOVERNOUR in CHIEF of the Province of QUEBECK.*

G. R.

GEORGE the THIRD, by the Grace of God, of Great Britain, France, and Ireland, King, Defender of the Faith, and so forth; to our trusty and well-beloved JAMES MURRAY, *Esquire, Greeting :*

Commission to be captain general and governour in chief of the province.

WE, reposing especial trust and confidence in the prudence, courage and loyalty of you, the said James Murray, of our especial grace, certain knowledge and mere motion, have thought fit to constitute and appoint, and by these presents do constitute and appoint you, the said James Murray, to be our captain general and governour in chief in and over our province of Quebeck in America ; bounded on the Labrador coast by the river St. John ; and from thence by a line drawn

Boundaries of the province.

* *Articles of capitulation granted by Sir Geoffry Amherst to the Canadians, upon the surrender of Montreal and the whole province of Canada to the British arms, in September*, 1760.

[N. B. *The articles that are here omitted are intirely of a temporary nature, and no way affect the present constitution of the province.*]

Art. IV. The militia, after being come out of the above towns, forts, and posts, shall return to their homes without being molested, on any pretence whatsoever, on account of their having carried arms. *Granted.*

Art. VII. The magazines, the artillery, firelocks, sabres, ammunition of war, and in general, every thing that belongs to his most Christian Majesty, as well in the towns of Montreal, and Trois Rivieres, as in the forts and posts mentioned in the third article, shall be delivered up, according to exact inventories, to the commissioners, who shall be appointed to receive the same in the name of his Britannic Majesty. Duplicates of the said inventories shall be given to the Marquis de Vaudreuil.

This is every thing that can be asked on this article.

Art. XII. The most convenient method that can be found shall be appointed to carry the Marquis de Vaudreuil, by the streightest passage, to the first sea port in France. The necessary accommodation shall be made for him, the Marquis de Vaudreuil, M. de Rigaud, governor of Montreal, and the suite of this general. This vessel shall be properly victualled at the expence of his Britannic Majesty; and the Marquis de Vaudreuil shall take with him his papers, without their being examined ; and his equipage, plate, baggage, and also those of his suite.

Granted, except the archieves, which shall be necessary for the government of the country.

Art. XXI. The English general shall also provide ships for carrying to France the officers of the supreme council, of justice, police, admiralty, and all other officers, having commissions or brevets from his most Christian majesty, for them, their families, servants, and equipages, as well as for the other officers : and they

drawn from the head of that river through the lake St. John to the ſouth end of the lake Nipiſſim, from whence the ſaid line croſſing the river St. Lawrence and the lake Champlain, in forty-five degrees of northern latitude, paſſes along the high lands which divide the rivers that empty themſelves into the ſaid river St. Lawrence from thoſe which fall into the ſea; and alſo along the north coaſt of the Baye des Chaleurs and the coaſt of the gulf of St. Lawrence to Cape Roſieres; and from thence croſſing the mouth of the river St. Lawrence by the weſt end of the iſland of Anticoſti, terminates at the aforeſaid river St. John: together with all the rights, members, and appurtenances whatſoever thereunto belonging.

The governour is to act according to the powers and directions of this commiſſion, and according to the King's inſtructions.

And we do hereby require and command you to do and execute all things in due manner that ſhall belong to your ſaid command and the truſt we have repoſed in you, according to the ſeveral powers and directions granted or appointed you by this preſent commiſſion and the inſtructions and authorities herewith given unto you, or by ſuch other powers, inſtructions, and authorities as ſhall at any time hereafter be granted or appointed under our ſignet and ſign manual, or by our order in

they ſhall likewiſe be victualled at the expence of his Britannic Majeſty. They ſhall, however, be at liberty to ſtay in the colony, if they think proper, to ſettle their affairs, or to withdraw to France, whenever they think fit.

Granted: but if they have papers relating to the government of the country, they are to be delivered to us.

Art. XXIV. The proviſions, and other kind of ſtores which ſhall be found in the magazines of the commiſſary, as well in the towns of Montreal, and of Trois Rivieres, as in the country, ſhall be preſerved to him, the ſaid proviſions belonging to him, and not to the King, and he ſhall be at liberty to ſell them to the French or Engliſh.

Every thing that is actually in the magazines, deſtined for the uſe of the troops, is to be delivered to the Engliſh commiſſary, for the King's forces.

India company.

Art. XXV. A paſſage to France ſhall likewiſe be granted on board of his Britannic Majeſty's ſhips, as well as victuals to ſuch officers of the India company, as ſhall be willing to go thither, and they ſhall take with them their families, ſervants, and baggage. The chief agent of the ſaid company, in caſe he ſhould chuſe to go to France, ſhall be allowed to leave ſuch perſon as he ſhall think proper till next year, to ſettle the affairs of the ſaid company, and to recover ſuch ſums as are due to them. The ſaid chief agent ſhall keep poſſeſſion of all the papers belonging to the ſaid company, and they ſhall not be liable to inſpection. *Granted.*

Art. XXVI. The ſaid company ſhall be maintained in the property of the ecarlatines and caſtors, which they may have in the town of Montreal; they ſhall not be touched under any pretence whatever, and the neceſſary facilities ſhall be given to the chief agent, to ſend, this year, his caſtors to France, on board his Britannic Majeſty's ſhips, paying the freight on the ſame footing as the Engliſh would pay it.

Granted, with regard to what may belong to the company, or to private perſons; but if his moſt Chriſtian majeſty has any ſhare in it, that muſt become the property of the King.

Art.

in our privy council, and according to such reasonable laws and statutes as shall hereafter be made and agreed upon by you with

Free exercise of the Roman Catholic religion.

Art. XXVII. The free exercise of the Catholic, Apostolic, and Roman religion, shall subsist intire; in such manner that all the states and the people of the towns and countries, places and distant posts, shall continue to assemble in the churches, and to frequent the sacraments as heretofore, without being molested in any manner directly or indirectly.

Payment of tithes and other church dues.

These people shall be obliged, by the English government, to pay to the priests, the tithes and all the taxes they were used to pay, under the government of his most Christian majesty.

Granted, as to the free exercise of their religion. The obligation of paying the tithes to the priests, will depend on the King's pleasure.

Art. XXVIII. The chapter, priests, curates, and missionaries, shall continue with an entire liberty, their exercise and functions of their cures, in the parishes of the towns and countries. *Granted.*

Power of the grand vicars to exercise ecclesiastical jurisdiction.

Art. XXIX. The grand vicars named by the chapter to administer to the diocese during the vacancy of the episcopal see, shall have liberty to dwell in the towns or country parishes as they shall think proper. They shall at all times be free to visit the different parishes of the diocese, with the ordinary ceremonies, and exercise all the jurisdiction they exercised under the French dominion. They shall enjoy the same rights in case of death of the future bishop, of which mention will be made in the following article.

Granted; except what regards the following article.

Nomination of the future bishops.

Art. XXX. If by the treaty of peace, Canada should remain in the power of his Britannic Majesty, his most Christian Majesty shall continue to name the bishop of the colony, who shall always be of the Roman communion, and under whose authority the people shall exercise the Roman religion. *Refused.*

Their power.

Art. XXXI. The bishop shall, in case of need, establish new parishes, and provide for the rebuilding of his cathedral and his episcopal palace; and, in the mean time, he shall have the liberty to dwell in the towns and parishes, as he shall judge proper. He shall be at liberty to visit his diocese with the ordinary ceremonies, and exercise all the jurisdiction which his predecessor exercised under the French dominion, save that an oath of fidelity, or a promise to do nothing contrary to his Britannic majesty's service, may be required of him.

This article is comprised under the foregoing.

Communities of nuns.

Art. XXXII. The communities of nuns shall be preserved in their constitutions and privileges. They shall continue to observe their rules. They shall be exempted from lodging any military, and it shall be forbid to trouble them in their religious exercises, or to enter their monasteries: safeguards shall even be given them if they desire them. *Granted.*

Jesuits, Recollet monks, and priests of Saint Sulpicius.

Art. XXXIII. The preceding article shall likewise be executed with regard to the communities of Jesuits and Recolets, and of the house of the priests of St. Sulpice at Montreal. These last, and the Jesuits, shall preserve their right to nominate to certain curacies and missions, as heretofore.

Refused till the King's pleasure be known.

Property of the religious communities and the priests.

Art. XXXIV. All the communities, and all the priests, shall preserve their moveables, the property and revenues of the seignories, and other estates which they possess in the colony, of what nature so ever they may be. And the same estates shall be preserved in their privileges, rights, honours and exemptions.

Granted.

Liberty to all the priests and monks to go to France, and to sell their estates.

Art. XXXV. If the canons, priests, missionaries, the priests of the seminary of the foreign missions, and of St. Sulpice, as well as the Jesuits and the Recolets, chuse to go to France, a passage shall be granted them in his Britannic Majesty's ships: and they shall all have leave to sell, in whole or in part, the estates and moveables which they possess in the colonies, either to the French or to the English, without the least hindrance or obstacle from the British government.

They

with the advice and consent of the council and assembly of our said province under your government, in such manner and form as is herein after expressed.

And

' They may take with them, or send to France, the produce, of what nature soever it be, of the said goods sold, paying the freight, as mentioned in the 26th article. And such of the said priests, who chuse to go this year, shall be victualled during the passage, at the expence of his Britannic Majesty; and shall take with them their baggage.

They shall be masters to dispose of their estates, and to send the produce thereof, as well as their persons, and all that belongs to them to France.

Art. XXXVI. If, by the treaty of peace, Canada remains to his Britannic Majesty, all the French, Canadians, Acadians, merchants, and other persons, who chuse to retire to France, shall have leave to do so from the English general, who shall procure them a passage. And, nevertheless, if, from this time to that decision, any French or Canadian merchants, or other persons, shall desire to go to France, they shall likewise have leave from the English general. Both the one and the other shall take with them their families, servants, and baggage. *Granted.*

Property of the laity of Canada.

Art. XXXVII. The lords of manors, the military and civil officers, the Canadians, as well in the towns as in the country, the French settled or trading in the whole extent of the colony of Canada, and all other persons whatsoever, shall preserve the entire peaceable property and possession of their goods, noble and ignoble, moveable and immovable, merchandizes, furs, and other effects, even their ships; they shall not be touched, nor the least damage done to them, on any pretence whatsoever. They shall have liberty to keep, let, or sell them, as well to the French as to the English, to take away the produce of them, in bills of exchange, furs, specie, or other returns, whenever they shall judge proper to go to France, paying their freight, as in the 26th article.

They shall also have the furs which are in the posts above, and which belong to them, and may be on the way to Montreal. And for this purpose they shall have leave to send, this year or the next, canoes, fitted out, to fetch such of the said furs as shall have remained in those parts.

Granted, as in the 26th article.

The Acadians.

Art. XXXVIII. All the people who have left Acadia, and who shall be found in Canada, including the frontiers of Canada on the side of Acadia, shall have the same treatment as the Canadians, and shall enjoy the same privileges.

The King is to dispose of his antient subjects: in the mean time they shall enjoy the same privilege as the Canadians.

Art. XXXIX. None of the Canadians, Acadians, or French, who are now in Canada, and on the frontiers of the colony, on the side of Acadia, Detroit, Michilimakinac, and other places and posts of the countries above, the married and unmarried soldiers, remaining in Canada, shall be carried or transported into the English colonies, or to Old England, and they shall not be troubled for having carried arms.

Granted; except with regard to the Acadians.

The Indians in alliance with the French.

Art. XL. The savages, or Indian allies of his most Christian Majesty, shall be maintained in the lands they inhabit, if they chuse to remain there; they shall not be molested on any pretence whatsoever, for having carried arms, and served his most Christian Majesty. They shall have, as well as the French, liberty of religion, and shall keep their missionaries. The actual vicars general, and the bishop, when the episcopal see shall be finished, shall have leave to send them new missionaries, when they shall judge it necessary.

Granted; except the last article, which has been already refused.

Continuance of the French laws.

Art. XLI. The French, Canadians, and Acadians, of what state and condition soever, who shall remain in the colony, shall not be forced to take arms against his most Christian Majesty, or his allies, directly or indirectly, on any oc-

casion

Oaths to be taken by the governor. And our will and pleasure is, that you, the said James Murray, do, after the publication of these our letters patent, and

casion whatsoever. The British government shall only require of them an exact neutrality.

They become subjects of the King.

Continuance of the French laws. Art. XLII. The French and Canadians shall contiue to be governed according to the custom of Paris, and the laws and usages established for this country; and they shall not be subject to any other imposts than those which were established under the French dominion.

Answered by the preceding articles, and particularly by the last.

Papers of the government. Art. XLIII. The papers of the government shall remain, without exception, in the power of the Marquis de Vaudreuil, and shall go to France with him. These papers shall not be examined on any pretence whatsoever.

Granted, with the reserve already made.

Papers of the intendant's office, and other public papers. Art. XLIV. The papers of the intendancy of the offices of comptroller of the marine, of the antient and new treasurers, of the King's magazines, of the office of the revenues, and forges of St. Maurice, shall remain in the power of M. Bigot, the intendant, and they shall be embarked for France in the same vessel with him. These papers shall not be examined.

The same as to this article.

The registers of the supreme council, and of the other courts of justice in the province. Art. XLV. The registers, and other papers of the supreme council of Quebeck, of the provost, and admiralty of the said city; those of the royal jurisdiction of Trois Rivieres, and of Montreal; those of the signeural jurisdictions of the colony; the minutes of the acts of the notaries of the towns and of the countries; and, in general, the acts, and other papers that may serve to prove the estates and fortunes of the citizens, shall remain in the colony, in the rolls of the jurisdictions on which these papers depend. *Granted.*

Liberty of trading as British subjects. Art. XLVI. The inhabitants and merchants shall enjoy all the privileges of trade, under the same favours and conditions, granted to the subjects of his Britannic Majesty, as well in the countries above, as in the interior of the colony. *Granted.*

Negroes and Panis slaves. Art. XLVII. The negroes and panis, of both sexes, shall remain in their quality of slaves, in the possession of the French and Canadians to whom they belong; they shall be at liberty to keep them in their service in the colony, or to sell them, and they may also continue to bring them up in the Roman religion.

Granted; except those who shall have been made prisoners.

Liberty to appoint attornies to take care of their affairs, and to sell their lands and goods, and send the produce to Old France. Art. XLVIII. The Marquis de Vaudreuil, the general and staff officers of the land forces, the governors and staff officers of the different places of the colony, the military and civil officers, and all other persons who shall leave the colony, or who are already absent, shall have leave to name and appoint attorneys to act for them, and in their names, in the administration of their effects, moveable and immoveable, until the peace. And if, by the treaty between the two crowns, Canada does not return under the French dominions, these officers, or other persons, or attorneys for them, shall have leave to sell their manors, houses, and other estates, their moveables and effects, &c. to carry away, or send to France the produce, either in bills of exchange, specie, furs, or other returns, as is mentioned in the 37th article. *Granted.*

Those whose goods have been damaged shall have justice. Art. XLIX. The inhabitants and other persons who shall have suffered any damage in their goods, moveable and immovaeble which remained at Quebeck, under the faith of the capitulation of that city, may make their representation to the British government, who shall render them due justice, against the person to whom it shall belong. *Granted.*

Art. L. and last. The present capitulation shall be inviolably executed in all its articles, and *bonâ fide* on both sides, notwithstanding any infraction and any other pretence, with regard to the preceding capitulations, and without making use of reprisals. *Granted.*

and after the appointment of our council for our ſaid province, in ſuch manner and form as is preſcribed in the inſtructions which

The Fourth Article of the Definitive Treaty of Peace, concluded between the KINGS of GREAT BRITAIN and FRANCE, on the 10th Day of February, 1763; containing the Ceſſion of Canada to the Crown of Great Britain.

HIS moſt Chriſtian Majeſty renounces all pretenſions which he has heretofore formed, or might form, to Nova Scotia, or Acadia, in all its parts, and guarantees the whole of it, and all its dependencies, to the King of Great Britain. *Ceſſion of Nova Scotia or Acadia.*

Moreover, his moſt Chriſtian Majeſty cedes and guarantees to his ſaid Britannic Majeſty, in full right, Canada, with all its dependencies, as well as the iſland of Cape Breton, and all the other iſlands and coaſts in the Gulf and River of St. Lawrence, and, in general, every thing that depends on the ſaid countries, lands, iſlands and coaſts, with the ſovereignty, property, poſſeſſion, and all rights acquired by treaty or otherwiſe, which the moſt Chriſtian King and the crown of France have had, till now, over the ſaid countries, iſlands, lands, places, coaſts, and their inhabitants, ſo that the moſt Chriſtian King cedes and makes over the whole to the ſaid King, and to the crown of Great Britain, and that in the moſt ample manner and form, without reſtriction, and without any liberty to depart from the ſaid guaranty, under any pretence, or to diſturb Great Britain in the poſſeſſions abovementioned. *Ceſſion of Canada and Cape Breton, and the iſles and coaſts in the gulf and river of St. Lawrence.*

His Britannic Majeſty, on his ſide, agrees to grant the liberty of the Catholic religion to the inhabitants of Canada: he will conſequently give the moſt effectual orders, that his new Roman Catholic ſubjects may profeſs the worſhip of their religion, according to the rites of the Romiſh church, as far as the laws of Great Britain permit. *Liberty of the Catholic religion to the Canadians.*

His Britannic Majeſty farther agrees, that the French inhabitants, or others, who had been the ſubjects of the moſt Chriſtian King in Canada, may retire with all ſafety and freedom wherever they ſhall think proper, and may ſell their eſtates, provided it be to ſubjects of his Britannic Majeſty, and bring away their effects, as well as their perſons, without being reſtrained in their emigration, under any pretence whatſoever, except that of debt, or of criminal proſecutions; the term limited for this emigration ſhall be fixed to the ſpace of eighteen months, to be computed from the day of the exchange of the ratification of the preſent treaty. *Liberty for the French King's ſubjects to retire within 18 months.*

The KING's PROCLAMATION of October 7, 1763.

G.R.

WHEREAS we have taken into our royal conſideration the extenſive and valuable acquiſitions in America, ſecured to our crown by the late definitive treaty of peace concluded at Paris the tenth day of February laſt; and being deſirous that all our loving ſubjects, as well of our kingdoms as of our colonies in America, may avail themſelves, with all convenient ſpeed, of the great benefits and advantages which muſt accrue therefrom to their commerce, manufactures, and navigation, we have thought fit, with the advice of our privy council, to iſſue this our royal proclamation, hereby to publiſh and declare to all our loving ſubjects, that we have, with the advice of our ſaid privy council, granted our letters patent under our great ſeal of Great Britain, to erect within the countries and iſlands ceded and confirmed to us by the ſaid treaty, four diſtinct and ſeparate governments, ſtiled and called by the names of Quebeck, Eaſt Florida, Weſt Florida, and Grenada, and limited and bounded as follows, viz.

Firſt, The government of Quebeck, bounded on the Labrador coaſt by the river St. John, and from thence by a line drawn from the head of that river, through the lake St. John, to the ſouth end of the lake Nipiſſim; from whence the ſaid line, croſſing the river St. Lawrence and the lake Champlain in forty-five degrees of north latitude, paſſes along the high lands, which divide the rivers that empty themſelves into the ſaid river St. Lawrence from thoſe which fall into the ſea; and *Government of Quebeck.*

which you will herewith receive, in the first place, take the oaths appointed to be taken by an act passed in the first year of

and also along the north coast of the *Baye des Chaleurs*, and the coast of the gulf of St. Lawrence to cape Rosieres, and from thence crossing the mouth of the river St. Lawrence by the west end of the island of Anticosti, terminates at the aforesaid river St. John.

Government of East Florida.

Secondly, The government of East Florida, bounded to the westward by the gulf of Mexico and the Apalachicola river; to the northward by a line drawn from that part of the said river where the Catahouchee and Flint rivers meet, to the source of St. Mary's river, and by the course of the said river to the Atlantick Ocean; and to the east and south by the Atlantick Ocean and the gulf of Florida, including all the islands within six leagues of the sea coast.

West Florida.

Thirdly, The government of West Florida, bounded to the southward by the gulf of Mexico, including all islands within six leagues of the coast from the river Apalachicola to lake Pontchartrain; to the westward by the said lake, the lake Maurepas and the river Mississippi; to the northward, by a line drawn east from that part of the river Mississippi which lies in thirty-one degrees of north latitude, to the river Apalachicola, or Catahouchee; and to the eastward by the said river.

Grenada.

Fourthly, the government of Grenada, comprehending the island of that name, together with the Grenadines, and the islands of Dominica, St. Vincent, and Tobago.

Enlargement of the government of Newfoundland.

And to the end that the open and free fishery of our subjects may be extended to, and carried on upon, the coast of Labrador and the adjacent islands, we have thought fit, with the advice of our said privy council, to put all that coast, from the river St. John's to Hudson's Streights, together with the Islands of Anticosti and Madelaine, and all smaller islands lying upon the said coast, under the care and inspection of our governour of Newfoundland.

Enlargement of Nova-Scotia.

We have also, with the advice of our privy council, thought fit to annex the islands of St. John and Cape Breton, or Isle Royale, with the lesser islands adjacent thereto, to our government of Nova Scotia.

Enlargement of Georgia.

We have also, with the advice of our privy council aforesaid, annexed to our province of Georgia all the lands lying between the rivers Atamaha and St. Mary's.

Power to the governours of the new governments to summon general assemblies.

And whereas it will greatly contribute to the speedy settling our said new governments, that our loving subjects should be informed of our paternal care for the security of the liberty and properties of those who are and shall become inhabitants thereof; we have thought fit to publish and declare, by this our proclamation, that we have, in the letters patent under our Great Seal of Great Britain, by which the said governments are constituted, given express power and direction to our governors of our said colonies respectively, that so soon as the state and circumstances of the said colonies will admit thereof, they shall, with the advice and consent of the members of our council, summon and call general assemblies within the said governments respectively, in such manner and form as is used and directed in those colonies and provinces in America which are under our immediate government; and we have also given power to the said governours, with the consent of our said council, and the representatives of the people, so to be summoned as aforesaid, to make, constitute and ordain laws, statutes and ordinances, for the public peace, welfare, and good government of our said colonies, and of the people and inhabitants thereof, as near as may be, agreeable to the laws of England, and under such regulations and restrictions as are used in the other colonies; *and in the mean time, and until such assemblies can be called as aforesaid, all persons inhabiting in, or resorting to, our said colonies, may confide in our royal protection for the enjoyment of the benefit of the laws of our realm of England; for which purpose we have given power under our great seal to the governours of our said colonies respectively, to erect and constitute, with the advice of our said councils respectively, courts of judicature and public justice within our said colonies, for the hearing and determining all causes, as well criminal as civil, according to law and equity, and as near as may be, agreeable to the laws of England, with liberty to all persons who may think themselves agrieved by the sentence of such courts, in all civil cases, to appeal, under the usual limitations and restrictions, to us in our privy council.*

Power to make laws, with the consent of such assemblies.

The laws of England shall be observed in mean time.

We

of the reign of King George the first, intituled, " *An act for the further security of his Majesty's person and government, and the succession*

Power to grant lands.

We have also thought fit, with the advice of our privy council as aforesaid, to give unto our governours and councils of our said three new colonies upon the continent full power and authority to settle and agree with the inhabitants of our said new colonies, or any other person who shall resort thereto, for such lands, tenements, and hereditaments as are now, or hereafter shall be, in our power to dispose of, and them to grant to any such person or persons, upon such terms and under such moderate quit-rents, services, and acknowledgments as have been appointed and settled in other colonies, and under such other conditions as shall appear to us to be necessary and expedient for the advantage of the grantees, and the improvement and settlement of our said colonies.

Lands to be granted to reduced officers and soldiers.

And whereas we are desirous, upon all occasions, to testify our royal sense and approbation of the conduct and bravery of the officers and soldiers of our armies, and to reward the same, we do hereby command and impower our governours of our several three new colonies, and other our governours of our several provinces on the continent of North America, to grant, without fee or reward, to such reduced officers and soldiers as have served in North America, during the late war, and are actually residing there, and shall personally apply for the same, the following quantities of land, subject at the expiration of ten years, to the same quit-rents as other lands are subject to in the province within which they are granted, as also subject to the same conditions of cultivation and improvement, viz.

To every person having the rank of a field officer, 5000 acres.

To every captain, 3000 acres.

To every subaltern or staff officer, 2000 acres.

To every non-commissioned officer, 200 acres.

To every private man, 50 acres.

And likewise to reduced officers of the navy.

We do likewise authorize and require the governours and commanders in chief of all our said colonies upon the continent of North America to grant the like quantities of land, and upon the same conditions, to such reduced officers of our navy of like rank as served on board our ships of war in North America at the times of the reduction of Louisbourg and Quebeck in the late war, and who shall personally apply to our respective governours for such grants.

And whereas it is just and reasonable, and essential to our interest, and the security of our colonies, that the several nations or tribes of Indians, with whom we are connected, and who live under our protection, should not be molested or disturbed in the possession of such parts of our dominions and territories as, not having been ceded to us, are reserved to them, or any of them, as their hunting grounds; we do therefore, with the advice of our privy council, declare it to be our royal will and pleasure, that no governour or commander in chief in any of our colonies of Quebeck, East Florida, or West Florida, do presume, upon any pretence whatever, to grant warrants of survey, or pass any patents, for lands beyond the bounds of their respective governments, as described in their commissions; as also that no governour or commander in chief of our other colonies or plantations in America do presume, for the present, and until our further pleasure be known, to grant warrants of survey, or pass patents, for any lands beyond the heads or sources of any of the rivers which fall into the Atlantic Ocean from the west or north-west, or upon any lands whatever, which, not having been ceded to or purchased by us as aforesaid, are reserved to the said Indians, or any of them.

No governor shall make grants of lands that have not been sold or ceded to the king by the Indians.

All the lands not included in the new governments shall be reserved for the Indians.

And we do further declare it to be our royal will and pleasure, for the present, as aforesaid, to reserve under our sovereignty, protection, and dominion, for the use of the said Indians, all the land and territories not included within the limits of our said three new governments, or within the limits of the territory granted to the Hudson's Bay company; as also all the land and territories lying to the westward of the sources of the rivers which fall into the sea from the west and north-west as aforesaid; and we do hereby strictly forbid, on pain of our displeasure, *succession of the crown in the heirs of the late princess Sophia, being protestants, and for extinguishing the hopes of the pretended prince of Wales, and his open and secret abettors;"* as also that you make and subscribe the declaration mentioned in an act of parliament made in the twenty-fifth year of the reign of King Charles the second, intituled, " *An act for preventing dangers*

pleasure, all our loving subjects from making any purchases or settlements whatsoever, or taking possession of any of the lands above reserved, without our especial leave and license for that purpose first obtained.

All persons settled on the grounds reserved for the Indians are required to retire therefrom.

And we do further strictly enjoin and require all persons whatsoever, who have either wilfully or inadvertently seated themselves upon any lands within the countries above described, or upon any other lands which, not having been ceded to or purchased by us, are still reserved to the said Indians as aforesaid, forthwith to remove themselves from such settlements.

And whereas great frauds and abuses have been committed in the purchasing lands of the Indians, to the great prejudice of our interests, and to the great dissatisfaction of the said Indians; in order therefore to prevent such irregularities for the future, and to the end that the Indians may be convinced of our justice and determined resolution to remove all reasonable cause of discontent, we do, with the advice of our privy council, strictly enjoin and require, that no private

No private private persons shall purchase any lands of the Indians.

person do presume to make any purchase from the said Indians of any lands reserved to the said Indians, within those parts of our colonies where we have thought proper to allow settlement; but if at any time any of the said Indians should be inclined to dispose of the said lands, the same shall be purchased only for us, in our name, in some public meeting or assembly of the said Indians, to be held for that purpose by the governour or commander in chief of our colony respectively within which they shall lie: and in case they shall lie within the limits of any proprietaries, conformable to such directions and instructions as we

The trade with the Indians shall be free to all the King's subjects.

or they shall think proper to give for that purpose. And we do, by the advice of our privy council, declare and enjoin, that the trade with the said Indians shall be free and open to all our subjects whatever; provided that every person who may incline to trade with the said Indians, do take out a license for carrying on such trade from the governour or commander in chief of any of our colonies respectively where such person shall reside, and also give security to observe such regulations as we shall at any time think fit, by ourselves or commissaries to be appointed for this purpose, to direct and appoint for the benefit of the said trade: and we do hereby authorize, enjoin and require the governours and commanders in chief of all our colonies respectively, as well those under our immediate government, as those under the government and direction of proprietaries, to grant such licences without fee or reward, taking especial care to insert therein a condition that such license shall be void, and the security forfeited, in case the person to whom the same is granted shall refuse or neglect to observe such regulations as we shall think proper to prescribe as aforesaid.

Power to seize and send back criminals, who fly from justice to the Indian country.

And we do further expressly enjoin and require all officers whatever, as well military as those employed in the management and direction of the Indian affairs within the territories reserved, as aforesaid, for the use of the said Indians, to seize and appehend all persons whatever, who standing charged with treason, misprison of treason, murder, or other felonies or misdemeanors, shall fly from justice and take refuge in the said territory, and to send them under a proper guard to the colony where the crime was committed of which they shall stand accused, in order to take their trial for the same.

Given at our court of St. James's, the 7th day of October 1763, in the third year of our reign.

GOD Save the KING.

which

which may happen from Popish recusants;" and likewise that you take the oath of office usually taken by our governours in the other colonies for the due execution of the office and trust of our captain general and governour in chief in and over our said province, and for the due and impartial administration of justice; and further, that you take the oath required to be taken by the governours of the plantations to do their utmost that the several laws relating to trade and plantations be duly observed: which said oaths and declarations our council of our said province, or any three of the members thereof, have hereby full power and authority, and are hereby required, to tender and administer to you.* Oath of Office. Oath to observe the laws relating to trade and plantations.

All

* *The following are oaths of allegiance and abjuration of the Pope's power, and the Pretender's right to the crown of Great Britain.*

I. *The* OATH *of* ALLEGIANCE.

I A. B. do sincerely promise and swear, that I will be faithful, and bear true allegiance, to his Majesty King George. So help me GOD.

II. *The OATH of ABJURATION of the POPE's POWER.*

I A. B. do swear, that I do from my heart abhor, detest, and abjure, as impious and heritical, that damnable doctrine and position, that princes excommunicated or deprived by the Pope, or any authority of the see of Rome, may be deposed or murdered by their subjects, or any other whatsoever.

And I do declare, that no foreign prince, person, prelate, state, or potentate, hath, or ought to have, any jurisdiction, power, superiority, pre-eminence, or authority, ecclesiastical or spiritual, within this realm. So help me GOD.

III. *The OATH of ABJURATION of the PRETENDER's RIGHT to the CROWN of GREAT BRITAIN.*

I A. B. do truly and sincerely acknowledge, profess, testify, and declare in my conscience, before God and the world, that our sovereign lord King George is the rightful King of this realm, and all other his Majesty's dominions thereunto belonging. *Acknowledgement of the King's right.*

And I do solemnly and sincerely declare, that I do believe in my conscience, that the person pretended to be prince of Wales, during the life of the late King James, and since his decease pretending to be, and taking upon himself the stile and title of, King of England, by the name of James the Third, or of Scotland, by the name of James the Eighth, or the stile and title of King of Great Britain, hath not any right or title whatsoever to the crown of this realm, or any other the dominions thereto belonging: and I do renounce, refuse, and abjure any allegiance or obedience to him. *Declaration against the Pretender's title; and renunciation of all allegiance to him.*

And I do swear, that I will bear faith and true allegiance to his Majesty King George, and him will defend, to the utmost of my power, against all traitorous conspiracies and attempts whatsoever, which shall be made against his person, crown, or dignity. And I will do my utmost endeavour to disclose and make known to his Majesty, and his successors, all treasons and traitorous conspiracies which I shall know to be against him, or any of them. *Promise to defend the King and disclose all conspiracies.*

And I do faithfully promise, to the utmost of my power, to support, maintain, and defend the succession of the crown against him the said James, and all other persons whatsoever, which succession, by an act, intituled, "An act for the further limitation of the crown and better securing the rights and liberties of the subject," is and stands limited to the princess Sophia, electoress and dutchess dowager of Hanover, and heirs of her body, being protestants. *Promise to maintain the Protestant succession.*

And

Oaths to be taken by the councillors, &c. of Montreal and Trois Rivieres.

All which being duly performed, you ſhall yourſelf adminiſter to each of the members of our ſaid council, and to the lieutenant-governours of Montreal and Trois Rivieres, the ſaid oaths mentioned in the ſaid act, intituled, "*An act for the further ſecurity of his Majeſty's perſon and government, and the ſucceſſion of the crown in the heirs of the late Princeſs Sophia, being Proteſtants, and for extinguiſhing the hopes of the pretended Prince of Wales, and his open and ſecret abettors*;" and alſo cauſe them to make and ſubſcribe the afore-mentioned declaration, and alſo ſhall adminiſter unto them the uſual oaths for the due execution of their places and truſt.

And

Sincerity of all theſe declarations, according to the plain meaning of the words.

And all theſe things I do plainly and ſincerely acknowledge and ſwear, according to theſe expreſs words by me ſpoken, and according to the plain and common ſenſe and underſtanding of the ſame words, without any equivocation, mental evaſion, or ſecret reſervation whatſoever. And I do make this recognition, acknowledgment, abjuration, renunciation, and promiſe, heartily, willingly, and truly, upon the true faith of a chriſtian. So help me GOD.

The foregoing oath of abjuration is that mentioned in the commiſſion above-recited of captain general and governour in chief of the province of Quebeck, granted to general Murray, which was paſſed in the life-time of the perſon pretending to be the ſon of King James the Second. Since the death of that Pretender it has been neceſſary to make ſome alteration in the wording of it; and this has been done by the ſtatute of the 6th year of the reign of his preſent Majeſty, by which the following oath of abjuration is enjoined to be taken inſtead of the former.

IV. *The OATH of ABJURATION of the RIGHT of any of the DESCENDANTS of the late King JAMES the SECOND to the CROWN of GREAT BRITAIN.*

Appointed by the ſtat. 6 Geo. III. cap. 53.

Acknowledgement of the King's right.

I A. B. do truly and ſincerely acknowledge, profeſs, teſtify, and declare, in my conſcience, before God and the world, that our ſovereign lord King George is the lawful and rightful King of this realm, and all other his Majeſty's dominions and countries thereunto belonging.

Declaration againſt the title of the deſcendants of the Pretender.

And I do ſolemnly and ſincerely declare, that I do believe in my conſcience, that not any of the deſcendants of the perſon who pretended to be prince of Wales during the life of the late King James the Second, and, ſince his deceaſe, pretended to be, and took upon himſelf the ſtile and title of, King of England, by the name of James the Third, or of Scotland, by the name of James the Eighth, or the ſtile and title of King of Great Britain, hath any right or title whatſoever to the crown of this realm, or any other the dominions thereunto belonging. And I do renounce, refuſe, and abjure any allegiance or obedience to any of them.

Promiſe to defend the King, and diſcloſe all conſpiracies.

And I do ſwear that I will bear faith and true allegiance to his Majeſty King George, and him will defend, to the utmoſt of my power, againſt all traitorous conſpiracies and attempts whatſoever, which ſhall be made againſt his perſon, crown, or dignity. And I will do my utmoſt endeavour to diſcloſe and make known to his Majeſty, and his ſucceſſors, all treaſons and traitorous conſpiracies which I ſhall know to be againſt him, or any of them.

Promiſe to maintain the Proteſtant ſucceſſion.

And I do faithfully promiſe, to the utmoſt of my power, to ſupport, maintain, and defend the ſucceſſion of the crown againſt the deſcendants of the ſaid James, and all other perſons whatſoever; which ſucceſſion, by an act, intituled, "An act for the further limitation of the crown, and better ſecuring the rights

" and

And we do further give and grant unto you, the said James Murray, full power and authority from time to time and at any time hereafter, by yourself, or by any other to be authorized by you in this behalf, to administer and give the oaths mentioned in the said act "*for the further security of his Majesty's person and government, and the succession of the crown in the heirs of the late princess Sophia, being protestants, and for extinguishing the hopes of the pretended prince of Wales, and his open and secret abettors,*" to all and every such person or persons as you shall think fit, who shall at any time or times pass into our said province, or shall be resident or abiding there.

Power for the governor to administer or impower others to administer the said oaths.

" and liberties of the subject," is and stands limited to the princess Sophia, electoress and dutchess dowager of Hanover, and the heirs of her body, being protestants.

And all these things I do plainly and sincerely acknowledge and swear, according to these express words by me spoken, and according to the plain common sense and understanding of the same words, without any equivocation, mental evasion, or secret reservation whatsoever. And I do make this recognition, acknowledgement, abjuration, renunciation and promise, heartily, willingly, and truly, upon the true faith of a christian.

Sincerity of all these declarations, according to the plain meaning of the words.

V. *The* DECLARATION *against* TRANSUBSTANTIATION.

Appointed by stat. 25 *Car.* II. *c.* 2. *sect.* 9.

I A. B. do declare, that I do believe that there is not any transubstantiation in the sacrament of the Lord's supper, or in the elements of bread and wine, at or after the consecration thereof by any person whatsoever.

Five years after the appointment of this decleration against transubstantiation, to wit, in the 30th year of the reign of King Charles the Second, and A. D. 1679, another declaration against some of the principal errors of popery was appointed to be taken on certain occasions, which is usually called The declaration against popery, and is as follows:

VI. *The* DECLARATION *against* POPERY.

Appointed to be taken in certain cases by the stat. 30 *Car.* II. *stat.* 2.

I A. B do solemnly and sincerely, in the presence of God, profess, testify, and declare, that I do believe, that in the sacrament of the Lord's supper there is not any transubstantiation of the elements of bread and wine into the body and blood of Christ, at or after the consecration thereof by any person whatsoever; and that the invocation or adoration of the Virgin Mary, or any other saint, and the sacrifice of the mass, as they are now used in the church of Rome, are superstitious and idolatrous.

No transubstantiation of the elements of bread and wine.

Saint worship, &c. idolatrous.

And I do solemnly, in the presence of God, profess, testify, and declare, that I do make this declaration, and every part thereof, in the plain and ordinary sense of the words read unto me, as they are commonly understood by English protestants, without any evasion, equivocation, or mental reservation whatsoever, and without any dispensation already granted me for this purpose by the Pope, or any other authority or person whatsoever, or without any hope of any such dispensation from any person or authority whatsoever, or without thinking that I am, or can be acquitted before God or man, or absolved of this declaration, or any part thereof, although the Pope, or any other person or persons, or power whatsoever, shall dispense with, or annul, the same, or declare that it was null and void from the beginning.

Sincerity of this declaration, according to the true meaning of the words.

Power to use public seal.

And we do hereby authorize and impower you to keep and use the public seal which will herewith be delivered to you, or shall be hereafter sent to you, for sealing all things whatsoever that shall pass the great seal of our province.

Power to call an assembly of the freeholders.

And we do hereby give and grant unto you, the said James Murray, full power and authority, with the advice and consent of our said council to be appointed as aforesaid, so soon as the situation and circumstances of our said province under your government will admit thereof, and when and as often as need shall require, to summon and call general assemblies of the freeholders and planters within your government, in such manner as you in your discretion shall judge most proper; or according to such further powers, instructions, and authorities, as shall be at any time hereafter granted or appointed you under our signet or sign manual, or by our order in our privy council.

The members to take the oaths appointed by stat. 1 Geo. I.

and the declaration against transubstantiation.

And our will and pleasure is, that the persons thereupon duly elected by the major part of the freeholders of the respective parishes or precincts, and so returned, shall, before their sitting, take the oaths mentioned in the said act, intituled, "*An act for the further security of his Majesty's person and government, and the succession of the crown in the heirs of the late princess Sophia, being protestants, and for extinguishing the hopes of the pretended prince of Wales, and his open and secret abettors*;" as also make and subscribe the fore-mentioned declaration; which oaths and declaration you shall commissionate fit persons under the public seal of that our province to tender and administer unto them; and, until the same shall be so taken and subscribed, no person shall be capable of sitting, though elected.

Power with consent of the council to make laws;

not repugnant to the laws of Great Britain.

And we do hereby declare, that the persons so elected and qualified shall be called The assembly of that our province of Quebeck; and that you, the said James Murray, by and with the advice and consent of our said council and assembly, or the major part of them, shall have full power and authority to make, constitute, and ordain, laws, statutes, and ordinances, for the public peace, welfare, and good government of our said province, and of the people and inhabitants thereof, and such others as shall resort thereunto, and for the benefit of us, our heirs and successors; which said laws, statutes, and ordinances are not to be repugnant, but, as near as may be, agreeable to the laws and statutes of this our kingdom of Great Britain.

Provided

Provided that all ſuch laws, ſtatutes, and ordinances, of what nature or duration ſoever they be, ſhall be, within three months, or ſooner, after the making thereof, tranſmitted to us, under our ſeal of our ſaid province, for our approbation or diſallowance of the ſame, as alſo duplicates thereof, by the next conveyance.

Laws ſo made ſhall be tranſmitted to England within 3 months.

And in caſe any, or all, of the ſaid laws, ſtatutes, and ordinances, not before confirmed by us, ſhall at any time be diſallowed and not approved, and ſo ſignified by us, our heirs and ſucceſſors, under our, or their, ſignet and ſign manual, or by order of our, or their, privy council, unto you, the ſaid James Murray, or to the commander in chief of our ſaid province for the time being, then ſuch and ſo many of the ſaid laws, ſtatutes, and ordinances as ſhall be ſo diſallowed and not approved, ſhall from thenceforth ceaſe, determine, and become utterly void and of no effect; any thing to the contrary thereof notwithſtanding.

If diſallowed by the king, they ſhall thence forth become void.

And to the end that nothing may be paſſed or done by our ſaid council or aſſembly to the prejudice of us, our heirs and ſucceſſors, we will and ordain that you the ſaid James Murray ſhall have and enjoy a negative voice in the making and paſſing all laws, ſtatutes, and ordinances as aforeſaid; and that you ſhall and may likewiſe from time to time, as you ſhall judge neceſſary, adjourn, prorogue, or diſſolve all general aſſemblies as aforeſaid.

Governor to have a negative voice.

And we do by theſe preſents give and grant unto you, the ſaid James Murray, full power and authority, with the advice and conſent of our ſaid council, to erect, conſtitute, and eſtabliſh ſuch and ſo many courts of judicature and public juſtice within our ſaid province under your government as you and they ſhall think fit and neceſſary, for the hearing and determining of all cauſes, as well criminal as civil, according to law and equity, and for awarding execution thereupon, with all reaſonable and neceſſary powers, authorities, fees, and privileges belonging thereto; as alſo to appoint and commiſſionate fit perſons in the ſeveral parts of your government to adminiſter the oaths mentioned in the aforeſaid act, intituled, "*An act for the further ſecurity of his Majeſty's perſon and government, and the ſucceſſion of the crown in the heirs of the late princeſs Sophia, being proteſtants, and for extinguiſhing the hopes of the pretended prince of Wales, and his open and ſecret abettors*; as alſo to tender and adminiſter the aforeſaid declaration to ſuch perſons belonging to the ſaid courts as ſhall be obliged to take the ſame.

Power with conſent of the council to erect courts of judicature; and to commiſſionate fit perſons to adminiſter the aforeſaid oaths to perſons belonging to ſuch courts.

Power to appoint judges, commissioners of Oyer and Terminer, justices of the peace, and other officers of justice.

And we do hereby grant unto you full power and authority to constitute and appoint judges, and, in cases requisite, commissioners of Oyer and Terminer, justices of the peace, and other necessary officers and ministers, in our said province, for the better administration of justice and putting the laws in execution; and to administer, or cause to be administered, unto them, such oath or oaths as are usually given for the due execution and performance of offices and places, and for clearing the truth in judicial causes.

Power to pardon crimes.

And we do hereby give and grant unto you full power and authority, when you shall see cause, or shall judge any offender or offenders in criminal matters, or for any fines or forfeitures due unto us, fit objects of our mercy, to pardon all such offenders, and remit all such offences, fines, and forfeitures, treason and wilful murder only excepted; in which cases you shall likewise have power, upon extraordinary occasions, to grant reprieves to the offender until, and to the intent that, our royal pleasure may be known therein.

Power to collate to ecclesiastical benefices.

And we do by these presents give and grant unto you full power and authority to collate any person or persons to any churches, chapels, or other ecclesiastical benefices within our said province, as often as any of them shall happen to be void.

Power to levy troops and employ them against enemies, pirates, and rebels;

And we do hereby give and grant unto you, the said James Murray, by yourself, or by your captains and commanders by you to be authorized, full power and authority to levy, arm, muster, command, and employ all persons whatsoever residing within our said province; and, as occasion shall serve, them to march, embark, or transport, from one place to another, for the resisting and withstanding of all enemies, pirates, and rebels, both at land and sea; and to transport such forces to any of our plantations in America, if necessity shall require, for the defence of the same against the invasion or attempts of any of our enemies; and such enemies, pirates, and rebels, if there should be occasion, to pursue and prosecute in or out of the limits of our said province: and, if it shall so please God, them to vanquish, apprehend, and take; and, being taken, according to law to put to death, or keep and preserve alive, at your discretion; and to execute martial law in time of invasion, war, or other times, when by law it may be executed; and to do and execute all and every other thing and things which to our captain general and governour in chief doth, or of right ought to belong.

and to execute martial law, in time of war.

And we do hereby give and grant unto you full power and authority, by and with the advice and consent of our said council,

council, to erect raise and build in our said province, such and so many forts, platforms, castles, cities, boroughs, towns, and fortifications, as you, by the advice aforesaid, shall judge necessary, and the same, or any of them, to fortify and furnish with ordinance, ammunition, and all sorts of arms fit and necessary for the security and defence of our said province; and by the advice aforesaid, the same again, or any of them, to demolish or dismantle as may be most convenient.

Power with consent of the council, to build forts and castles; and to fortify and furnish them with arms, &c. and to demolish or dismantle them.

And forasmuch as divers mutinies and disorders may happen by persons shipped and employed at sea during the time of war, and to the end that such as shall be shipped and employed at sea during the time of war may be better governed and ordered, we hereby give and grant unto you, the said James Murray, full power and authority to constitute and appoint captains, lieutenants, masters of ships, and other commanders and officers; and to grant to such captains, lieutenants, masters of ships, and other commanders and officers, commissions to execute the law martial, during the time of war, according to the directions of an act passed in the twenty-second year of the reign of our late royal grandfather, intitled, "*An act for amending, explaining, and reducing into one act of parliament, the laws relating to the government of his Majesty's ships, vessels, and forces by sea*;" and to use such proceedings, authorities, punishments, corrections, and executions upon every offender or offenders, who shall be mutinous, seditious, disorderly, or any way unruly, either at sea, or during the time of their abode or residence in any of the ports, harbours, or bays in our said province, as the case shall be found to require, according to martial law; and the said directions, during the the time of war, as aforesaid.

Power to appoint captains and other officers of ships, and to grant them commissions to excute the law martial.

Provided, that nothing herein contained shall be construed to the enabling you, or any by your authority to hold plea, or have any jurisdiction of any offence, cause, matter, or thing committed or done upon the high sea, or within any of the havens, rivers, or creeks of our said province under your government, by any captain, commander, lieutenant, master, officer, seaman, soldier, or person whatsoever, who shall be in actual service and pay, in or on board any of our ships of war, or other vessels acting by immediate commission or warrant from our commissioners for executing the office of high admiral of Great Britain, or from our high admiral of Great Britain for the time being, under the seal of our admiralty; but that such captain, commander, lieutenant, master, officer, seaman, soldier, or other person,

This shall not affect any officers, &c. on board ships commissioned by the admiralty, when they commit offences either on the high sea, or in any river, creek, or haven.

But these persons shall be tried for such offences either by commissions under the great seal of Great Britain or by commission from the admiralty.

person so offending, shall be left to be proceeded against, and tried, as their offences shall require, either by commission under our great seal of this kingdom, as the statute of the twenty-eighth of Henry VIII. directs; or by commission from our said commissioners for executing the office of high admiral of Great Britain, or from our high admiral of Great Britain for the time being, according to the aforementioned act, intituled, "*An act for amending, explaining, and reducing into one act of parliament, the laws relating to the government of his Majesty's ships, vessels, and forces by sea*;" and not otherwise.

But for offences committed on shore, those persons shall be tried and punished according to the laws of the place where the offence shall be committed.

Provided nevertheless, that all disorders and misdemeanors committed on shore by any captain, commander, lieutenant, master, officer, seaman, soldier, or other person whatsoever belonging to any of our ships of war, or other vessels acting by immediate commission or warrant from our commissioners for executing the office of high admiral of Great Britain, or from our high admiral of Great Britain for the time being, under the seal of our admiralty, may be tried and punished according to the laws of the place, where any such disorders, offences, and misdemeanors shall be committed on shore; notwithstanding such offender be in our actual service, and borne in our pay on board any of our ships of war, or other vessels acting by our immediate commission, or warrant from our commissioners for executing the office of high admiral of Great Britain, or from our high admiral of Great Britain for the time being, as aforesaid, so as he shall not receive any protection for the avoiding of justice for such offences committed on shore from any pretence of his being employed in our service at sea.

Power with consent of the council to dispose of public monies, for support of government.

And our further will and pleasure is, that all public monies raised, or which shall be raised, by any act hereafter to be made within our said province, be issued out by warrant from you, by and with the advice and consent of our council, as aforesaid, for the support of the government, and not otherwise.

Power with consent of the council, to grant lands.

And we likewise give and grant unto you full power and authority, by and with the advice and consent of our said council, to settle and agree with the inhabitants of our said province for such lands, tenements, and hereditaments, as now are, or hereafter shall be in our power to dispose of, and them to grant to any person or persons upon such terms and under such moderate quit-rents, services, and acknowledgements to be thereupon reserved unto us, as you, with the

the advice aforeſaid, ſhall think fit; which ſaid grants are to paſs, and be ſealed by our public ſeal of our ſaid province, and being entered upon record by ſuch officer or officers as ſhall be appointed thereunto, ſhall be good and effectual in law againſt us, our heirs and ſucceſſors.

Grants to be under the public ſeal and to be regiſtered.

Provided the ſame be conformable to the inſtructions herewith delivered to you, or to ſuch other inſtructions as may hereafter be ſent you under our ſignet and ſign manual, or by our order in our privy council; which inſtructions, or any articles contained therein, or any ſuch order made in our privy council, ſo far as the ſame ſhall relate to the granting of lands as aforeſaid, ſhall from time to time be publiſhed in the province, and entered on record in like manner as the ſaid grants are hereby directed to be entered.

Theſe grants muſt be made conformable to the King's inſtructions.

And we do hereby give you the ſaid James Murray, full power and authority to order fairs, marts, and markets; and alſo ſuch and ſo many ports, harbours, bays, havens, and other places for the conveniency or ſecurity of ſhipping, and for the better loading and unloading of goods and merchandizes, in ſuch and ſo many places, as by you, with the advice and conſent of our ſaid council, ſhall be thought fit and neceſſary.

Power, with conſent of the council to appoint fairs, &c.

And we do hereby require and command all officers and miniſters, civil and military, and all other inhabitants of our ſaid province to be obedient, aiding, and aſſiſting unto you, the ſaid James Murray, in the execution of this our commiſſion, and of the powers and authorities therein contained; and in caſe of your death or abſence from our ſaid province and government, to be obedient, aiding, and aſſiſting, as aforeſaid, to the commander in chief for the time being, to whom we do therefore by theſe preſents give and grant all and ſingular the powers and authorities herein granted to be by him executed and enjoyed, during our pleaſure, or until your arrival within our ſaid province.

All officers, &c. to aid and aſſiſt the governor or lieut.gov. in the execution of his commiſſion.

And in caſe of your death or abſence from our ſaid province, our will and pleaſure is, that our lieutenant governor of Montreal or Trois Rivieres, according to the priority of their commiſſions of lieutenant governour, do execute our ſaid commiſſion with all the powers and authorities therein mentioned, as aforeſaid. And in caſe of the death or abſence of our lieutenant governours of Montreal and Trois Rivieres from our ſaid province, and that there ſhall be no perſon within our ſaid province appointed by us to be lieutenant governour or commander in chief of our ſaid province,

Who to be commander in chief of the province, in caſe of the death or abſence of the governor.

vince, our will and pleaſure is, that the eldeſt councillor, who ſhall be, at the time of your death or abſence, reſiding within our ſaid province, ſhall take upon him the adminiſtration of the government, and execute our ſaid commiſſion and inſtructions, and the ſeveral powers and authorities therein contained, in the ſame manner and to all intents and purpoſes, as other our governour or commander in chief ſhould or ought to do, in caſe of your abſence, or until your return, or in all caſes until our further pleaſure be known

This office to be held during the King's pleaſure.

And we do hereby declare, ordain, and appoint, that you, the ſaid James Murray, ſhall and may hold, execute, and enjoy the office and place of our captain general and governor in chief, in and over our ſaid province of Quebeck, and all the territories dependent thereon, with all and ſingular the powers and authorities hereby granted unto you, for and during our will and pleaſure. In witneſs whereof we have cauſed theſe our letters to be made patent; witneſs ourſelf at Weſtminſter, the twenty-firſt day of November, in the fourth year of our reign.

By writ of privy ſeal. (Signed) YORKE & YORKE.

Recorded at the Treaſury chambers, Whitehall, the 28th day of November, 1763.

(Signed) T. TOMKYNS.

Recorded in the Regiſter's office in Quebeck, the 7th day of June, 1766.

(Signed) J. GOLDFRAP, D. Regr.

COMMIS-

COMMISSION of VICE-ADMIRAL.

GEORGE the THIRD, by the Grace of God, of Great-Britain, France, and Ireland, King, Defender of the Faith, to our beloved JAMES MURRAY, *Esquire, our Captain General and Governour in Chief in and over our Province of Quebeck, in America, Greeting:*

WE, confiding very much in your fidelity, care, and circumspection in this behalf, do, by these presents, which are to continue during our pleasure only, *constitute and depute* you, the said James Murray, Esquire, our captain general and governour in chief aforesaid, *our vice-admiral, commissary, and deputy in the office of vice-admiralty* in our province of Quebeck aforesaid, and territories thereon depending, and in the maritime parts of the same and thereto adjoining whatsoever; with power of taking and receiving all and every the fees, profits, advantages, emoluments, commodities, and appurtenances whatsoever due and belonging to the said office of Vice-Admiral, Commissary, and Deputy in our province of Quebeck, and territories depending thereon, and maritime parts of the same and adjoining to them whatsoever, according to the ordinances and statutes of our high court of admiralty in England.

Commission to be vice-admiral, commissary, & deputy in the office of vice-admiralty in the province of Quebeck.

And we do hereby remit and grant unto you, the aforesaid James Murray, Esquire, our power and authority in and throughout our province of Quebeck afore-mentioned, and territories thereof, and maritime parts whatsoever of the same and thereto adjacent, *and also throughout all and every the sea-shores, public streams, ports, fresh-water rivers, creeks, and arms as well of the sea as of the rivers and coasts whatsoever of our said province of Quebeck*, and territories dependent thereon, and maritime parts whatsoever of the same and thereto adjacent, as well within liberties and franchises as without; to take *cognizance of, and proceed in, all civil and maritime causes, and in complaints, contracts, offences, or suspected offences, crimes, pleas, debts, exchanges, accounts, charter-partys, agreements, suits, trespasses, injuries, extortions, and demands, and business civil and maritime whatsoever*, commenced or to be commenced between merchants, or between owners and proprietors of ships and other vessels, and merchants or others whomsoever with such owners and proprietors of ships and all other vessels

To what places the vice-admiral's jurisdiction shall extend.

In what causes.

Between what persons.

whatſoever, employed or uſed within the maritime juriſdiction of our vice-admiralty of our ſaid province of Quebeck, and territories depending on the ſame, or between any other perſons whomſoever, had, made, begun, or contracted for any matter, thing, cauſe, or buſineſs whatſoever, done or to be done within our maritime juriſdiction aforeſaid, together with all and ſingular their incidents, emergencies, dependencies, annexed or connexed cauſes whatſoever or howſoever, and ſuch cauſes, complaints, contracts, and other the premiſes above ſaid, or any of them, which may happen to ariſe, be contracted, had, or done, to hear and determine according to the rigbts, ſtatutes, laws, ordinances, and cuſtoms anciently obſerved.

And moreover, in all and ſingular complaints, contracts, agreements, cauſes, and buſineſſes, civil and maritime, to be performed beyond the ſea, or contracted there, howſoever ariſing or happening; and alſo in all and ſingular other cauſes and matters, which in any manner whatſoever touch or any way concern, or anciently have and do, or ought to, belong unto the maritime juriſdiction of our aforeſaid vice-admiralty in our ſaid province of Quebeck, and territories thereon depending, and maritime parts thereof and to the ſame adjoining whatſoever; and generally in all and ſingular all other cauſes, ſuits, crimes, offences, exceſſes, injuries, complaints, miſdemeanours, or ſuſpected miſdemeanours, treſpaſſes, regrating, foreſtalling and maritime buſineſſes whatſoever, throughout the places aforeſaid, within the maritime juriſdiction of our vice-admiralty of our province of Quebeck aforeſaid, and territories thereon depending by ſea or water, or the banks or ſhores of the ſame, howſoever done, committed, perpetrated, or happening.

To enquire by a jury of ſuch matters as of right, and by ancient laws and uſages, ought to be enquired of; and of wreck of the ſea, and the goods of traitors and felons;

And alſo to enquire by the oaths of honeſt and lawful men of our ſaid province of Quebeck, and territories dependent thereon, and maritime parts of the ſame and adjoining to them whatſoever, dwelling both within liberties and franchiſes and without, as well of all and ſingular ſuch matters and things which of right, and by the ſtatutes, laws, ordinances, and the cuſtoms anciently obſerved were wont and ought to be enquired after, as of wreck of the ſea, and of all and ſingular the goods and chattels of whatſoever traitors, pirates, manſlayers, and felons howſoever offending within the maritime juriſdiction of our vice-admiralty of our province of Quebeck afore-mentioned, and territories thereunto belonging, and of the goods, chattels, and debts of all and ſingu-

ſingular their maintainors, acceſſaries, counſellors, abettors, or aſſiſtants whomſoever.

And alſo of the goods, debts, and chattels of whatſoever perſon or perſons felons of themſelves, by what means or howſoever coming to their death within our aforeſaid maritime juriſdiction, whereſoever any ſuch goods, debts, and chattels, or any part thereof, by ſea, water, or land in our ſaid province of Quebeck, and territories thereon dependent, and maritime parts of the ſame and thereto adjacent whatſoever, as well within liberties and franchiſes as without, have been or ſhall be found forfeited, or to be forfeited, or in being.

and of the goods of felons of themſelves.

And moreover, as well of the goods, debts, and chattels of whatſoever other traitors, felons, and manſlayers whereſoever offending, and of the goods, debts, and chattels of their maintainors, acceſſaries, counſellors, abettors, or aſſiſtants, as of the goods, debts, or chattels of all fugitives, perſons convicted, attainted, condemned, outlawed, or howſoever put, or to be put, in exigent for treaſon, felony, manſlaughter, or murder, or any other offence or crime whatſoever; and alſo concerning goods waived, flotſon, jetſon, lagon, ſhares and treaſure found or to be found; deodands, and of the goods of all others whatſoever taken or to be taken as derelict, or by chance found, or howſoever due or to be due; and of all other caſualties, as well in, upon, or by the ſea and ſhores, creeks or coaſts of the ſea, or maritime parts, as in, upon, or by all freſh waters, ports, public ſtreams, rivers, or creeks, or places overflown whatſoever within the ebbing and flowing of the ſea or high water, or upon the ſhores and banks of any of the ſame within our maritime juriſdiction aforeſaid, howſoever, whenſoever, or by what means ſoever ariſing, happening, or proceeding, or whereſoever ſuch goods, debts, and chattels, or other the premiſes, or any parcel thereof, may or ſhall happen to be met with or found within our maritime juriſdiction aforeſaid.

Alſo of goods waived, flotſon, jetſon, lagon deodands, derelicts, and other caſualties, upon the ſea, or ſea-coaſts, or freſh-water rivers, as far as the tide flows.

And alſo concerning anchorage, laſtage, and ballaſt of ſhips, and of fiſhes royal, namely ſturgeons, whales, porpoiſes, dolphins, kiggs, and grampuſſes, and generally of all other fiſhes whatſoever which are of a great or very large bulk or fatneſs, anciently by right, or cuſtom, or any way appertaining or belonging to us.

Alſo of anchorage, laſtage, ballaſt, and fiſhes royal.

And to aſk, require, levy, take, collect, receive, and obtain for the uſe of us, and to the office of our high admiral of Great Britain aforeſaid for the time being, to keep and preſerve the ſaid wreck of the ſea, and the goods, debts, and chattels of all and ſingular other the premiſes, together with all and all manner of fines, mulcts, iſſues, forfeitures, amerciaments, ran-

Power to receive and preſerve to the King's uſe all the profits above-mentioned; and all fines imposed by any court of admiralty held in this province, and recognizances forfeited therein: ransoms, and recognizances whatsoever, forfeited, or to be forfeited, and pecuniary punishments for trespasses, crimes, injuries, extortions, contempts, and other misdemeanors whatsoever, howsoever imposed or inflicted, or to be imposed or inflicted, for any matter, cause, or thing whatsoever in our said province of Quebeck, and territories thereunto belonging, and maritime parts of the same and thereto adjoining, in any court *of our admiralty there held, or to be held,* presented, or to be presented, assessed, brought, forfeited, or adjudged; and also all amerciaments, issues, fines, perquisites, mulcts, and pecuniary punishments whatsoever, and forfeitures of all manner of recognizances, before you *or your lieutenant, deputy or deputies,* in our said province of Quebeck, and territories thereunto belonging, and maritime parts of the same and thereto adjacent whatsoever, happening, or imposed, or to be imposed or inflicted, or by any means assessed, presented, forfeited, or adjudged, or howsoever, by reason of the premises, due or to be due in that behalf to us, or to our heirs and successors.

and to take recognizances and bonds, for the King's use, or that of private subjects: and to award execution upon them; and to arrest ships, goods, and persons for causes arising within the maritime jurisdiction: And further, to take all manner of recognizances, cautions, obligations and stipulations, as well to our use as at the instance of any party's, for agreements, or debts, or other causes whatsoever, and to put the same into execution, and to cause and command them to be executed; *and also to arrest, and cause and command to be arrested,* according to the civil and maritime laws and ancient customs of our said court, all ships, persons, things, goods, wares, and merchandizes, for the premises, and every of them, and for other causes whatsoever concerning the same, wheresoever they shall be met with or found throughout our said province of Quebeck, and territories thereunto belonging, and maritime parts thereof and thereto adjoining, as well within liberties and franchises as without; and likewise for all other agreements, causes, or debts, howsoever contracted or arising, so that the goods or persons may be found within our jurisdiction aforesaid.

and to hear and determine the said causes, with all the matters incident thereto: And to hear, examine, discuss, and finally determine the same, with their emergencies, dependencies, incidents, annexed and connexed causes and businesses whatsoever; together with all other causes civil and maritime, and complaints, contracts, and all and every the respective premises whatsoever above expressed, according to the laws and customs aforesaid, and by all other lawful ways, means, and methods, according to the best of your skill and knowledge.

and to compel persons to appear and answer: And to compel all manner of persons in that behalf, as the case shall require, to appear and to answer, with power of of uſing any temporal correction, and of inflicting any other penalty or mulct, according to the laws and cuſtoms aforeſaid.

And to do and adminiſter juſtice according to the right order and courſe of law, ſummarily and plainly, looking only into the truth of the facts.

And to fine, correct, puniſh, chaſtiſe, reform, and to impriſon, and cauſe and command to be impriſoned, in any gaols, being within our province of Quebeck aforeſaid, and territories thereunto belonging, the parties guilty, and the contemners of the law and juriſdiction of our admiralty aforeſaid, and violaters, uſurpers, delinquents, and contumacious abſenters, maſters of ſhips, mariners, rowers, fiſhermen, ſhipwrights, and other workmen and artificers whatſoever, exerciſing any kind of maritime affairs, according to the rights, ſtatutes, laws, and ordinances, and cuſtoms anciently obſerved; and to deliver and abſolutely diſcharge, and cauſe and command to be diſcharged, whatſoever perſons impriſoned in ſuch caſes, who are to be delivered.

and to fine and impriſon the parties that ſhall be found guilty and to deliver and diſcharge from priſon perſons impriſoned for the ſame, when they ought to be ſo diſcharged:

And to preſerve, or cauſe to be preſerved, the public ſtreams, ports, rivers, freſh waters, and creeks whatſoever, within our maritime juriſdiction aforeſaid, in what place ſoever they be in our province of Quebeck aforeſaid, and territories thereunto belonging, and maritime parts of the ſame and thereto adjacent whatſoever, as well for the preſervation of our navy royal, and of the fleets and veſſels of our kingdom and dominions aforeſaid, as of whatſoever fiſhes increaſing in the rivers and places aforeſaid.

and to preſerve public ſtreams, ports, and rivers:

And alſo to keep, and cauſe to be executed and kept, in our ſaid province of Quebeck, and territories thereunto belonging, and maritime parts thereof and thereto adjacent whatſoever, the rights, ſtatutes, laws, ordinances, and cuſtoms anciently obſerved.

And to do, exerciſe, expedite, and execute all and ſingular other things in the premiſes, and every of them, as they by right, and according to the laws and ſtatutes, ordinances and cuſtoms aforeſaid, ſhould be done.

And moreover, to reform nets too cloſe, and other unlawful engines or inſtruments whatſoever for the catching of fiſhes whereſoever, by ſea, or public ſtreams, ports, rivers, freſh waters, or creeks whatſoever, throughout our province of Quebeck aforeſaid, and territories depending thereon, and maritime parts of the ſame and thereto adjacent, uſed or exerciſed within our maritime juriſdiction aforeſaid whereſoever.

and to reform nets that are too cloſe, and other unlawful engines for catching fiſh;

And

and to punish those who make use of them:

And to punish and correct the exercisers and occupiers thereof, according to the statutes, laws, ordinances, and customs aforesaid.

and to pronounce sentences in all causes relating to the sea, and put the same in execution:

And to pronounce, promulge, and interpose all manner of sentences and decrees, and to put the same in execution; with cognizance and jurisdiction of whatsoever other causes, civil and maritime, which relate to the sea, or which any manner of ways respect or concern the sea, or passage over the same, or naval or maritime voyages, or our said maritime jurisdiction, or the places or limits of our said admiralty, and cognizance afore-mentioned, and all other things done or to be done.

and to proceed in the said causes:

With power also to proceed in the same, according to the statutes, laws, ordinances, and customs aforesaid anciently used, as well of mere office mixt or promoted, as at the instance of any party, as the case shall require and seem convenient: and likewise with cognizance and decision of wreck of the sea, and of the death, drowning, and view of dead bodies of all persons howsoever killed, or drowned, or murdered, or which shall happen to be killed, drowned, or murdered, or by any other means come to their death in the sea or public streams, ports, fresh waters, or creeks whatsoever, within the flowing of the sea and high-water mark throughout our aforesaid province of Quebeck, and territories thereunto belonging, and maritime parts of the same and thereto adjacent, or elsewhere within our maritime jurisdiction aforesaid.

and to have cognizance of wreck of the sea, and view of dead bodies of persons coming to their deaths upon the sea or within the maritime jurisdiction:

Together with the congnizance of mayhem in the aforesaid places, within our maritime jurisdiction aforesaid, and flowing of the sea and water there happening; with power also of punishing all delinquents in that kind, according to the exigences of the law and customs aforesaid.

and to have cognizance of mayhem within the maritime jurisdiction.

And to do, exercise, expedite, and execute all and singular other things which in and about the premises only shall be necessary or thought meet, according to the rights, statutes, laws, ordinances, and customs aforesaid.

Power to make one or more deputies, and to appoint inferior officers.

With power of deputing and surrogating in your place for the premises one or more deputy or deputies, as often as you shall think fit; and also with power from time to time of naming, appointing, ordaining, assigning, making, and constituting whatsoever other necessary, fit, and convenient officers and ministers under you for the said office and execution thereof in our said province of Quebec, and territories thereunto belonging, and maritime parts of the same and thereto adjacent whatsoever.

Saving always the right of our high court of admiralty of England, and also of the judge and registrar of the said court, from

whom,

whom, or either of them, it is not our intention in any thing to derogate by these presents; and saving to every one who shall be wronged or grieved by any definitive sentence or interlocutory decree which shall be given *in the vice-admiralty court of our province of Quebeck* aforesaid, and territories thereunto belonging, the right of appealing to our aforesaid high court of admiralty of England.

Saving the right of the high court of admiralty, &c. and saving the right of appealing thereto.

Provided nevertheless, and under this express condition, that if you, the aforesaid James Murray, esquire, our captain general and governour in chief, shall not yearly (to wit) at the end of every year, between the feast of St. Michael the archangel and All Saints, duly certify, and cause to be effectually certified (if you shall be thereunto required) to us, and our lieutenant official, principals and commissary general and special, and judge and president of the high court of our admiralty of England aforesaid, all that which from time to time by virtue of these presents you shall do and execute, collect, or receive in the premises, or any of them, together with your full and faithful account thereupon, to be made in an authentic form, and sealed with the seal of our office remaining in your custody, that from thence and after default therein these our letters patent of the office of vice-admiralty aforesaid, as above granted, shall be null and void, and of no force or effect.

Proviso that the vice-admiral shall yearly certify under the seal of his office the proceedings had in his court to the judge of admiralty: and upon default made herein these letters patent shall be void.

Further we do, in our name, command all and singular our governours, justices, mayors, sheriffs, captains, marshals, bailiffs, keepers of all our gaols and prisons, constables, and all other our officers and faithful liege subjects whatsoever, and every of them, as well within liberties and franchises as without, that in and about the execution of the premises, and every of them, they be aiding, favouring, assisting, submissive, and yield obedience in all things as is fitting to you, the aforesaid James Murray, esquire, our captain general and governour in chief of our province of Quebeck aforesaid, *and to your deputy whomsoever*, and to all other officers by you appointed, and to be appointed, of *our said vice-admiralty in our province of Quebeck* aforesaid, and territories thereunto belonging, and maritime parts of the same and thereto adjoining, under pain of the law, and the peril which will fall thereon.

All officers, civil and military, and all other subjects whatsoever, are enjoined to be assisting to the vice-admiral and his deputies in the execution of this office.

Given at London in the high court of our admiralty of England aforesaid, under the great seal thereof, the nineteenth day of March, in the year of our Lord one thousand seven hundred and sixty-four, and of our reign the fourth.

(Signed.) GODF. LEE FARRANT, Registrar.

An Abſtract of the Contents of the Act of Parliament, intitled, "*An Act for making more effectual proviſion for the government of the province of Quebeck in North America.*" *Paſſed in June*, 1774.

Art. I. THE preamble ſtates, in the firſt place, that his Majeſty had, by his royal proclamation of October 7, 1763, declared the proviſions which he had made in reſpect to the ſeveral countries, territories, and iſlands in America, that had been ceded to him by the definitive treaty of peace, concluded at Paris on the 10th day of February, 1763.

Art. II. Then it ſtates, in the ſecond place, that by the arrangements made by the ſaid proclamation, a very great part of the country ſo ceded was left without any proviſion for the adminiſtration of civil government therein, notwithſtanding there were ſeveral colonies and ſettlements of the ſubjects of France in the ſaid part, who claimed to remain therein under the faith of the aforeſaid treaty.

Art. III. Then it ſtates, in the third place, that there were other parts of the countries ſo ceded to his Majeſty, in which ſedentary fiſheries had been eſtabliſhed and carried on by the ſubjects of France, inhabitants of the country called Canada, under grants made by the French government; and that theſe parts of the ceded countries had, by the ſaid proclamation of October 7, 1763, been anexed to the government of Newfoundland, and thereby made ſubject to regulations inconſiſtent with the nature of ſuch fiſheries.

Art. IV. Then comes the firſt enacting clauſe of the act, which directs that all the interior parts of North America contained between the weſtern boundaries of the old Engliſh colonies there, the rivers Ohio and Miſſiſſippi, and the territories of the Hudſon's Bay company; and likewiſe all the coaſt of Labrador, on the north ſide of the gulph of St. Lawrence, which had lately made part of the government of Newfoundland; ſhall be annexed to, and make part of, the province of Quebeck, during the King's pleaſure.

Art. 5. To the next enacting clauſe there is a preamble, in which it is declared, that the proviſions made by the proclamation above-mentioned in reſpect to the civil government of the ſaid province of Quebeck, and the powers and authorities

rities given to the governor and other civil officers of the ſaid province, by the grants and commiſſions iſſued in conſequence thereof, *had been found upon experience, to be inapplicable to the ſtate and circumſtances of the ſaid province*, the inhabitants whereof had amounted at the conqueſt to above ſixty-five thouſand perſons profeſſing the religion of the church of Rome, and enjoying an eſtabliſhed form of conſtitution and ſyſtem of laws, by which their perſons and property had been protected, governed, and ordered, for a long ſeries of years, from the firſt eſtabliſhment of the ſaid province of Canada.

Art. VI. Then comes the enacting clauſe itſelf, and enacts that the ſaid proclamation of October, 1763, and the commiſſion under the authority of which the government of the ſaid province was at that time adminiſtered, and all the ordinances that had been made by the governour and council of Quebeck, concerning the civil government and adminiſtration of juſtice in the ſaid province, and all commiſſions to judges and other officers thereof, ſhould become null and void on the 1ſt day of May, 1775.

Art. VII. The next clauſe relates to religion. It enacts in the firſt place, that his Majeſty's Roman-catholick ſubjects in the ſaid province of Quebeck, may enjoy the free exerciſe of their religion, ſubject to the King's ſupremacy, as declared and eſtabliſhed by an act made in the firſt year of the reign of queen Elizabeth.

Art. VIII. This clauſe concerning religion enacts, in the ſecond place, that the clergy of the ſaid church of Rome, may hold, receive, and enjoy their accuſtomed dues and rights, with reſpect to ſuch perſons only as ſhall profeſs the Roman-catholick religion.

Art. IX. Then follows a proviſoe that it ſhall be lawful for the King, his heirs and ſucceſſors, out of the reſt of the ſaid accuſtomed dues and rights, to make ſuch proviſion for the encouragement of the proteſtant religion, and for the maintainance and ſupport of a proteſtant clergy in the ſaid province, as he or they ſhall think expedient.

Art. X. After this follows a ſecond proviſo, by which all Roman-catholicks in the province, whether prieſts or laymen are exempted from the obligation of taking the oath of ſupremacy required by the aforeſaid ſtatute of the firſt of Elizabeth, or the oath of abjuration of the Pope's eccleſiaſtical authority, which has been ſubſtituted inſtead of the former by a ſtatute of king William. And in lieu of the ſaid oath againſt the Pope's authority, thoſe perſons who would by the ſaid ſtatutes of queen Elizabeth and king William have been obliged to take the ſame, (as all perſons holding eccleſiaſtical benefices, or temporal employments, would have been) ſhall, if they are Roman-catholicks, take the following oath of allegiance to the King's Majeſty, to wit,

"I *A. B.* do ſincerely promiſe and ſwear that I will be "faithful and bear true allegiance to his Majeſty king George, "and him will defend to the utmoſt of my power againſt "all traiterous conſpiracies and attempts whatſoever, which "ſhall be made againſt his perſon, crown, and dignity. And "I will do my utmoſt endeavour to diſcloſe and make known "to his Majeſty, his heirs and ſucceſſors, all treaſons and "traiterous conſpiracies, and attempts, which I ſhall know "to be againſt him or any of them. And all this I do ſwear "without any equivocation, mental evaſion, or ſecret reſer-"vation, and renouncing all pardons and diſpenſations from "any power or perſon whomſoever to the contrary.

"So help me God."

And if they ſhall neglect or refuſe to take the ſaid oath of allegiance, they ſhall incur the ſame penalties and forfeitures, and be liable to the ſame diſabilities as are appointed by the ſaid act of the firſt of queen Elizabeth, for neglecting or refuſing to take the oath of ſupremacy required by that ſtatute.

Art. XI. The next clauſe of this act conſiſts of two parts; in the firſt place, it confirms to all his Majeſty's Canadian ſubjects in the province of Quebeck, except the religious orders and communities, the enjoyment of their property and poſſeſſions, together with all cuſtoms and uſages relative thereto, and all other their civil rights, in as large, ample, and beneficial a manner as if the aforeſaid proclamation, commiſſions, ordinances, and other acts and inſtruments, had not been made, and as may conſiſt with their allegiance to his Majeſty, and ſubjection to the Crown and Parliament of Great-Britain.

Art. XII. And in the ſecond place, it directs that in all matters of controverſy relative to property and civil rights, reſort ſhall be had to the laws of Canada, as the rule for the deciſion of the ſame; and that all cauſes that ſhall hereafter be inſtituted in any of the courts of juſtice that ſhall be eſtabliſhed in the ſaid province, ſhall with reſpect to ſuch property and rights, be determined agreeably to the ſaid laws and cuſtoms of Canada, until they ſhall be varied or altered by any ordinances that ſhall hereafter be paſſed in the ſaid province by the governour and legiſlative council of the ſame,

to

to be appointed in the manner herein after mentioned. This clause is followed by two provisoes.

Art. XIII. By the first provisoe it is provided, that nothing in this act shall extend to any lands that have been granted by his Majesty, or that shall be granted hereafter by his Majesty, or his heirs and successors, to be holden in common soccage.

Art. XIV. The second provisoe, impowers all his Majesty's subjects in the said province to devise both their goods and their lands by their last will and testament in the manner they shall think proper, such will being executed either according to the laws of Canada, or according to the forms prescribed by the laws of England.

Art. XV. The next clause directs that the criminal law of England, (which it states to have been uniformly administered in the province for the last nine years, with the general approbation of the inhabitants thereof) shall continue to be observed in the said province; subject to such alterations and amendments as shall be made therein from time to time, by the governour and legislative council of the said province.

Art. XVI. Then comes the important clause for establishing a legislative council in the province. To this clause there is a preamble, which states two things; first, that it may be necessary to make regulations for the good government of the province of Quebeck, the occasion, of which cannot now be foreseen, nor without much delay and inconvenience be provided for, without entrusting the authority to make them, for a certain time, and under proper restrictions, to persons resident in the said province. And secondly that it is at present inexpedient to call an assembly.

Art. XVII. After this preamble, this clause enacts, that it shall be lawful for the King's Majesty, his heirs and successors, by warrant under his or their signet or sign manual, and with, the advice of the privy council, to constitute and appoint a council for the affairs of the said province of Quebeck, to consist of such persons resident in the same as his Majesty shall be pleased to appoint, being not fewer than seventeen, nor more than twenty-three; and upon the death, removal, or absence of any of the members of the said council, in like manner to constitute and appoint so many other persons as shall be necessary to supply the vacancies: and that this council, so appointed and nominated, or the major part thereof, shall have power and authority, with the consent of the governour for the time being, to make ordinances for the peace, welfare, and good government of the said province.

Art. XVIII. Then follows a provisoe that this legislative council shall not be impowered to lay any taxes or duties within the said province, except only such rates and taxes as the inhabitants of any town or district within the said province may be authorized by the said council to assess, levy, and apply within the said town or district, for the purpose of making roads, erecting and repairing publick buildings, or for any other purpose respecting the local convenience and œconomy of such town or district.

Art. XIX. Then follows a second provisoe, that the ordinances made by this legislative council shall, within six months after the passing of them, be transmitted to his Majesty for his royal approbation: and, if his Majesty shall think fit to disallow them, and make an order in his privy council for that purpose, they shall cease and become void in the said province from the time that his Majesty's order in council thereupon shall be promulgated. And no time is fixed for such disallowance: so that it seems to follow that his Majesty may disallow the said ordinances at the distance of forty or fifty years after they shall have been passed, or at any other distance of time whatsoever.

Art. XX. Then follows a third provisoe, that no ordinance touching religion, or by which any punishment may be inflicted greater than fine or imprisonment for three months, shall be of any force or effect, until the same shall have received his Majesty's approbation.

Art. XXI. Then comes the fourth and last provisoe to this clause concerning the legislative council, to wit, that no ordinance shall be passed at any meeting of this council where less than a majority of the whole council shall be present, or at any time, except between the first day of January, and the first day of May, unless upon some urgent occasion; in which case every member of the said council resident at Quebeck, or within fifty miles thereof, shall be personally summoned by the governour to attend the same.

Then comes a clause which enacts, that nothing in the said act contained shall extend to prevent his Majesty from erecting, by his letters patent under the great seal of Great-Britain, such courts of criminal, civil, and ecclesiastical jurisdiction in the said province of Quebeck, and appointing the judges and officers thereof, as his Majesty shall think necessary and proper for the circumstances of the said province.

Lastly, there is a general provisoe to the whole act, which declares that it is not intended to repeal the acts of Parliament relating

relating to the trade of the American colonies; but that all thoſe acts, and likewiſe all other acts of Parliament heretofore made concerning thoſe colonies, ſhall be of force in the ſaid province of Quebeck.

This is a pretty full and faithful abſtract of the famous Quebeck act.

A Commiſſion of his late Majeſty King GEORGE the Second to Sir DANVERS OSBORN, Baronet, to be Captain-General and Governour in Chief in and over the Province of NEW YORK in AMERICA, in the Year 1754.

GEORGE the SECOND, by the Grace of God, of Great Britain, France, and Ireland, King, Defender of the Faith, and ſo forth; To our truſty and well-beloved Sir Danvers Oſborn, *Baronet, greeting.*

WHEREAS we did by our letters patent under our great ſeal of Great-Britain, bearing date at Weſtminſter the third day of July in the fifteenth year of our reign, conſtitute and appoint the honourable George Clinton, eſq. captain-general and governour in chief in and over our province of New York and the territories depending thereon in America for and during our will and pleaſure, as by the ſaid recited letters patent (relation being thereunto had) may more fully and at large appear: Now know you that we have revoked and determined, and by theſe preſents do revoke and determine, the ſaid recited letters patent and every clauſe, article, and thing therein contained.

Revocation of the patent of the laſt governour.

And further know you that we, repoſing eſpecial truſt and confidence in the prudence, courage, and loyalty of you, the ſaid Sir Danvers Oſborn, of our eſpecial grace, certain knowledge, and meer motion, have thought fit to conſtitute and appoint you, the ſaid Sir Danvers Oſborn, to be our captain-general and governour in chief in and over our province of New York and the territories depending thereon in America: and we do hereby require and command you to do and execute all things in due manner that ſhall belong unto your ſaid command and the truſt we have repoſed in you, according to the ſeveral powers and directions granted or appointed you by this preſent commiſſion and inſtructions herewith

Appointment of the new governour.

herewith given you, or by *such further powers**, instructions and authorities, *as shall at any time hereafter be granted or appointed you under our signet and sign manual*, or by our order in our privy council, and according to such reasonable laws and statutes as now are in force or hereafter shall be made and agreed upon by you, with the advice and consent of our council and the assembly of our said province under your government, in such manner and form as is herein after expressed.

Oaths to be taken by the governour.

Those appointed by stat. 1. Geo. I.

The declaration against transubstantiation, mentioned in stat. 25 Car. II.

Oath of office.

And our will and pleasure is, that you the said Sir Danvers Osborn, after the publication of these our letters patent, do in the first place take the oaths appointed to be taken by an act passed in the first year of our late royal father's reign, intitled, "*An act for the further security of his Majesty's person and government, and the succession of the crown in the heirs of the late princess Sophia, being protestants, and for extinguishing the hopes of the pretended prince of Wales and his open and secret abettors*," as also that you make and subscribe the declaration mentioned in an act of Parliament made in the twenty-fifth year of the reign of king Charles the Second, intitled, "*An act for preventing dangers which may happen from popish recusants*:" and likewise that you take the usual oath for the due execution of the office and trust of our captain-general and governour in chief in and over our said province of New York and the territories depending thereon, for the due and impartial adminstration of justice; and further that you take the oath required to be taken by governours of plantations to do their utmost that the several laws relating to trade and the plantations be observed: which said oaths and declaration our council in our said province, or any three of the members thereof, have hereby full power and authority, and are required, to tender and administer unto you, and in your absence to our lieutenant-governour, if there be any upon the place; all which being duly performed you shall administer unto each of the members of our said council, as also to our lieutenant-governour, if there be any upon the place, the oaths mentioned in the said act, intitled, "*An act for the further security of his Majesty's person and government, and the succession of the crown in the heirs of the late princess Sophia, being protestants, and for extinguishing the hopes of the pretended*

Oath concerning the law of trade.

Oaths to be taken by members of the council.

Those appointed by stat. 1. Geo. I.

* *Quere*, Whether such powers would be legally delegated by an instrument under the King's signet and sign manual?

pretended prince of Wales and his open and secret abettors;" as also to cause them to make and subscribe the afore-mentioned declaration, and to adminster to them the oath for the due execution of their places and trusts.

Declaration above-mentioned.
Oath of office.

And we do hereby give and grant unto you full power and authority to suspend any of the members of our said council from sitting, voting, or assisting therein, if you shall find just cause for so doing; and, if there shall be any lieutenant-governour, him likewise to suspend from the execution of his command, and to appoint another in his stead until our pleasure be known. And if it shall at any time happen that by the death, departure out of our said province, or suspension of any of our said councillors, or otherwise, there shall be a vacancy in our said council (any three whereof we do hereby appoint to be a quorum) our will and pleasure is, that you signify the same unto us by the first opportunity, that we may under our signet and sign manual constitute and appoint others in their stead. But, that our affairs may not suffer at that distance for want of a due number of councillors, if ever it should happen that there be less than seven of them residing in our said province, we do hereby give and grant unto you, the said Sir Danvers Osborn, full power and authority to chuse as many persons out of the principal freeholders, inhabitants thereof, as will make up the full number of our said council to be seven and no more; which persons so chosen and appointed by you shall be to all intents and purposes councillors in our said province, until either they shall be confirmed by us, or that, by the nomination of others by us under our sign manual and signet, our said council shall have seven or more persons in it.

Power of suspending the members of the council.

Power to appoint new councillors till the number of the members is seven.

And we do hereby give and grant unto you full power and authority, with the advice and consent of our said council, from time to time as need shall require, to summon and call general assemblies of the said freeholders and planters within your government according to the usage of our province of New York. And our will and pleasure is, that the persons thereupon duly elected by the major part of the freeholders of the respective counties and places and so returned, shall, before their sitting, take the oaths mentioned in the said act intituled, "*An act for the further security of his Majesty's person and government, and the succession of the crown in the heirs of the late princess Sophia, being protestants, and for extinguishing the*

Power with the consent of the council, to call an assembly.

Oaths to be taken by the members thereof.

the hopes of the pretended prince of Wales and his open and secret abettors;" as also make and subscribe the afore-mentioned declaration (which oaths and declaration you shall commissionate fit persons under our seal of New York to tender and administer unto them): and until the same shall be so taken and subscribed, no person shall be capable of sitting, though elected.

The declaration afore-mentioned is to be subscribed by them.

Name of members so elected and qualified.

And we do hereby declare that the persons so elected and qualified shall be called and deemed *The general assembly* of that our province and the territories depending thereon.

Power to make laws,

which shall not be repugnant to the laws of Great-Britain.

And you, the said Sir Danvers Osborn, by and with the consent of our said council and assembly, or the major part of them respectively, shall have full power and authority to make, constitute, and ordain, laws, statutes. and ordinances for the public peace, welfare, and good government of our said province, and of the people and inhabitants thereof, and such others as shall resort thereto, and for the benefit of us, our heirs, and successors: which said laws, statutes, and ordinances are not to be repugnant, but, as near as may be, agreeable to the laws and statutes of this our kingdom of Great Britain.

The laws so made shall be transmitted to England within 3 months.

Provided that all such laws, statutes, and ordinances, of what nature or duration soever, be, within three months or sooner after the making thereof, transmitted unto us under our seal of New York for our approbation or disallowance of the same; as also duplicates thereof by the next conveyance.

If they are at any time after disallowed by the king, they shall thenceforth become void.

And in case any or all of the said laws, statutes, and ordinances, being not before confirmed by us, shall at any time be disallowed and not approved, and so signified by us, our heirs, or successors, under our, or their, sign manual and signet, or by order of our, or their, privy council unto you, the said Sir Danvers Osborn, or to the commander in chief of our said province for the time being; then such and so many of the said laws, statutes, and ordinances as shall be so disallowed and not approved, shall from thenceforth cease, determine, and become utterly void and of none effect; any thing to the contrary thereof notwithstanding.

The governour shall have a negative voice against both council and assembly.

And to the end that nothing may be passed or done by our said council or assembly to the prejudice of us, our heirs, or successors, we will and ordain that you, the said Sir Danvers Osborn, shall have and enjoy a negative voice in the making and passing of all laws, statutes, and ordinances as aforesaid: and you shall and may likewise from time to time,

as

as you ſhall judge it neceſſary, adjourn, prorogue, and diſſolve all general aſſemblies as aforeſaid.

Power of adjourning, proroguing, and diſſolving the aſſembly; and to keep and uſe the public ſeal.

And our further will and pleaſure is, that you ſhall and may uſe and keep the public ſeal of our ſaid province of New York for ſealing all things whatſoever that paſs the great ſeal of our ſaid province under your government.

Power to adminiſter, or to authorize others to adminiſter, the oaths appointed by ſtat. 1 Geo. I.

And we do further give and grant unto you, the ſaid Sir Danvers Oſborn, full power and authority from time to time and at any time hereafter, by yourſelf, or by any other to be authorized by you in that behalf, to adminiſter and give the afore-mentioned oaths to all and every ſuch perſon and perſons as you ſhall think fit, who ſhall at any time or times paſs into our ſaid province or ſhall be reſident or abiding there.

Power with the conſent of the council, to erect courts of judicature, and to commiſſionate fit perſons to adminiſter the oaths appointed by ſtat. 1 Geo. I. and the declaration, againſt tranſubſtantiation, to perſons belonging to ſuch courts.

And we do further by theſe preſents give and grant unto you, the ſaid Sir Danvers Oſborn, full power and authority, with the advice and conſent of our ſaid council, to erect, conſtitute, and eſtabliſh ſuch and ſo many courts of judicature and public juſtice within our ſaid province under your government, as you and they ſhall think fit and neceſſary for the hearing and determining of all cauſes, as well criminal as civil, according to law and equity, and for awarding execution thereupon, with all reaſonable and neceſſary powers, authorities, fees, and privileges belonging thereunto: as alſo to appoint and commiſſionate fit perſons in the ſeveral parts of your government to adminiſter the oaths mentioned in the aforeſaid act, intitled, "*An act for the further ſecurity of his Majeſty's perſon and government, and the ſucceſſion of the crown in the heirs of the late princeſs Sophia, being proteſtants, and for extinguiſhing the hopes of the pretended prince of Wales and his open and ſecret abettors*;" as alſo to tender and adminiſter the aforeſaid declaration, unto ſuch perſons belonging to the ſaid courts as ſhall be obliged to take the ſame.

Power to appoint judges, commiſſioners of Oyer and Terminer, juſtices of the peace, and other officers of juſtice.

And we do hereby authorize and impower you to conſtitute and appoint judges, and in caſes requiſite commiſſioners of Oyer and Terminer, juſtices of the peace, and other neceſſary officers and miniſters in our ſaid province for the better adminiſtration of juſtice and putting the laws in execution, and to adminiſter, or cauſe to be adminiſtered, unto them ſuch oath or oaths as are uſually given for the due execution and performance of offices and places, and for the clearing of truth in judicial cauſes.

Power to pardon crimes.

And we do hereby give and grant unto you full power and authority, where you ſhall ſee cauſe or ſhall judge any offender or offenders in criminal matters, or for any fines or forfeitures due unto us, fit objects of our mercy, to pardon all such offenders, and to remit all such offences, fines, and forfeitures, treason and wilful murder only excepted, in which cases you shall likewise have power upon extraordinary occasions to grant reprieves to the offenders until, and to the intent that, our royal pleasure may be known therein.

Power to collate to ecclesiastical benefices.

And we do by these presents authorize and impower you to collate any person or persons to any churches, chapels, or other ecclesiastical benefices within our said province and territories aforesaid, as often as any of them shall happen to be void.

Power to levy troops, and employ them against enemies, pirates, and rebels;

And we do hereby give and grant unto you, the said Sir Danvers Osborn, by yourself or by your captains and commanders by you to be authorized, full power and authority to levy, arm, muster, command, and employ all persons whatsoever residing within our said province of New York and other the territories under your government, and, as occasion shall serve, to march them from one place to another, or to embark them, for the resisting and withstanding of all enemies, pirates, and rebels, both at sea and land; and to transport such forces to any of our plantations in America, if necessity shall require, for the defence of the same against the invasions or attempts of any of our enemies; and such enemies, pirates, and rebels, if there shall be occasion, to pursue and prosecute in or out of the limits of our said province and plantations, or any of them, and if it shall so please God, them to vanquish, apprehend, and, being taken, either according to law to put to death or keep and preserve alive at your discretion: and to execute martial law in time of invasion, or other times when by law it may be executed: and to do and execute all and every other thing and things which to our captain-general and governour in chief doth, or ought of right to belong.

and to execute martial law in time of war.

Power, with the consent of the council, to build forts and castles;

And we do hereby give and grant unto you full power and authority, by and with the advice and consent of our said council, to erect, raise, and build in our said province of New York and the territories depending thereon, such and so many forts and platforms, castles, cities, boroughs, towns, and fortifications as you, by the advice aforesaid, shall judge necessary; and the same, or any of them, to fortify and furnish with ordnance, ammunition, and all sorts of arms fit and necessary for the security and defence of our said province; and, by the advice aforesaid, the same again, or any

and to fortify and furnish them with arms, &c.

of

of them, to demolish or dismantle, as may be most convenient.

And forasmuch as divers mutinies and disorders may happen by persons shipped and employed at sea during the time of war; and to the end that such as shall be shipped and employed at sea during time of war may be better governed and ordered, we do hereby give and grant unto you, the said Sir Danvers Osborn, full power and authority to constitute and appoint captains, lieutenants, masters of ships, and other commanders and officers, and to grant to such captains, lieutenants, masters of ships, and other commanders and officers, commissions to execute the law martial during the time of war, according to the directions of two acts, the one passed in the thirteenth year of the reign of king Charles the Second, intituled, "*An act for the establishing articles and orders for the regulating and better government of his Majesty's navies, ships of war, and forces by sea;*" and the other passed in the eighteenth year of our reign, intituled, "*An act for the further regulating and better government of his Majesty's navies, ships of war, and forces by sea, and for regulating proceedings upon courts martial in the sea service;*" and to use such proceedings, authorities, punishments, corrections, and executions upon any offender or offenders who shall be mutinous, seditious, disorderly, or any way unruly, either at sea, or during the time of their abode and residence in any of the ports, harbours, or bays of our said province and territories, as the case shall be found to require, according to the martial law and the said directions during the time of war as aforesaid.

Provided that nothing herein contained shall be construed to the enabling you, or any by your authority, to hold plea or have any jurisdiction of any offences, cause, matter, or thing, committed or done upon the high sea or within any of the havens, rivers, or creeks of our said province and territories under your government, by any captain, commander, lieutenant, master, officer, seaman, soldier, or other person whatsoever, who shall be in our actual service and pay, in or on board any of our ships of war, or other vessels, acting by immediate commission or warrant from our commissioners for executing the office of our high admiral, or from our high admiral of Great Britain for the time being, under the seal of our admiralty; but that such captain, commander, lieutenant, master, officer, seaman, soldier, or other person so offending shall be left to be proceeded against and tried

and to demolish or dismantle them.

Power to appoint captains and other officers of ships, and to grant them commissions to execute the law martial according to the stat. 13 Car. II. and 18 Geo. II.

This shall not affect any officers, &c. on board ships commissioned by the admiralty, when they commit offences either on the high sea, or in any river, creek, or haven.

But these persons shall be tried for such offences either

by commissions under the great seal of Great Britain or by commission from the admiralty.

tried as their offences shall require, either by commission under our great seal of Great-Britain as the statute of the twenty-eighth of Henry the Eighth directs, or by commission from our said commissioners for executing the office of our high admiral, or from our high admiral of Great Britain for the time being, according to the afore-mentioned acts.

But for offences committed on shore, those persons shall be tried and punished according to the laws of the place where the offence shall be committed.

Provided nevertheless, that all disorders and misdemeanours committed on shore by any captain, commander, lieutenant, master, officer, seaman, soldier, or other person whatsoever belonging to any of our ships of war or other vessels, acting by immediate commission or warrant from our said commissioners for executing the office of our high admiral, or from our high admiral of Great Britain for the time being, under the seal of our admiralty, may be tried and punished according to the laws of the place where any such disorder, offence, and misdemeanour shall be committed on shore, notwithstanding such offenders be in our actual service and borne in our pay on board any such our ships of war, or other vessels acting by immediate commission or warrant from our said commissioners for executing the office of our high admiral, or from our high admiral of Great Britain for the time being, as aforesaid, so as he shall not receive any protection for the avoiding of justice for such offences committed on shore from any pretence of his being employed in our service at sea.

Power, with the consent of the council, to dispose of all public monies raised in the province for the support of the government.

And our further will and pleasure is, that all public monies raised or which shall be raised by any act to be hereafter made within our said province and other the territories depending thereon, be issued out by warrant from you, by and with the advice and consent of our council, and disposed of by you for the support of the government, and not otherwise.

Power, with the consent of the council, to grant lands.

And we do hereby likewise give and grant unto you full power and authority, by and with the advice and consent of our said council, to settle and agree with the inhabitants of our province and territories aforesaid for such lands, tenements, and hereditaments as now are, or hereafter shall be, in our power to dispose of, and them to grant to any person or persons upon such terms and under such moderate quit-rents, services, and acknowledgments, to be thereupon reserved unto us, as you, by and with the advice aforesaid, shall think fit: which said grants are to pass and be sealed by our seal of New York, and, being entered upon record by such officer or officers as are or shall be appointed thereunto, shall

The grants to be under the public seal to be registered.

ſhall be good and effectual in law againſt us, our heirs, and ſucceſſors.

And we do hereby give you, the ſaid Sir Danvers Oſborn, full power to order and appoint fairs, marts, and markets, as alſo ſuch and ſo many ports, harbours, bays, havens, and other places for the convenience and ſecurity of ſhipping, and for the better loading and unloading of goods, and merchandizes, as by you, with the advice and conſent of our ſaid council, ſhall be thought fit and neceſſary.

Power, with the conſent of the council, to appoint fairs, &c.

And we do hereby require and command all officers and miniſters civil and military, and all other inhabitants of our ſaid province and territories depending thereon, to be obedient, aiding, and aſſiſting unto you, the ſaid Sir Danvers Oſborn, in the execution of this our commiſſion and the powers and authorities herein contained; and in caſe of your death or abſence out of our ſaid province and territories depending thereon, to be obedient, aiding and aſſiſting unto ſuch perſon as ſhall be appointed by us to be our lieutenant-governour or commander in chief of our ſaid province; to whom we do therefore by theſe preſents give and grant all and ſingular the powers and authorities herein granted, to be by him executed and enjoyed during our pleaſure or until your arrival within our ſaid province and territories.

All officers, &c. are to be aiding and aſſiſting to the governour in the execution of this commiſſion; to the lieutenant-governour or commander in chief for the time being.

And if, upon your death or abſence out of our ſaid province and territories depending thereon, there be no perſon upon the place commiſſionated or appointed by us to be our lieutenant-governour or commander in chief of our ſaid province, our will and pleaſure is, that the eldeſt counſellor, whoſe name is firſt placed in our ſaid inſtructions to you, and who ſhall at the time of your death or abſence be reſiding within our ſaid province of New York, ſhall take upon him the adminiſtration of the government, and execute our ſaid commiſſion and inſtructions and the ſeveral powers and authorities therein contained, in the ſame manner and to all intents and purpoſes as other our governour and commander in chief of our ſaid province ſhould or ought to do in caſe of your abſence until your return, or in all caſes until our further pleaſure be known therein.

In caſe of the death or abſence of the governour, and if there be no lieutenant-governour in the province, the command ſhall devolve upon the eldeſt counſellor.

And we do hereby declare, ordain, and appoint that you, the ſaid Sir Danvers Oſborn, ſhall and may hold, execute, and enjoy the office and place of our captain-general and governour in chief in and over our province of New York and the territories depending thereon, together with all and ſingular

This office of capt. gen. and gov. in chief of the ſd. province ſhall be held during the King's pleaſure.

gular the powers and authorities hereby granted unto you, for and during our will and pleasure.

And whereas there are divers colonies adjoining to our province of New York, for the defence and security whereof it is requisite that due care be taken in time of war; we have therefore thought it necessary for our service, and for the better protection and security of our subjects inhabiting those parts, to constitute and appoint, and we do by these presents constitute and appoint, you, the said Sir Danvers Osborn, to be our captain-general and commander in chief of the militia and of all the forces by sea and land within our colony of Connecticut, and of all our forts and places of strength within the same; and for the better ordering, governing and ruling our said militia and all our forces, forts, and places of strength within our said colony of Connecticut, we do hereby give and grant unto you, the said Sir Danvers Osborn, and, in your absence, to our commander in chief of our province of New York, all and every the like powers as in these presents are before granted and recited for the ruling, governing, and ordering our militia and all our forces, forts, and places of strength within our province of New York, to be exercised by you, the said Sir Danvers Osborn, and in your absence from our territories and dominion of New York, by our commander in chief of our province of New York, within our said colony of Connecticut, for and during our pleasure.

Grant of the office of capt gen. and commander in chief of the militia and other forces both by sea and land of the colony of Connecticut.

In witness whereof we have caused these our letters to be made patent.

Witness ourself at Westminster the first day of August in the twenty-seventh year of our reign.

By writ of privy seal,
YORKE and YORKE.

The

The first Charter, granted by King Charles II. *to the Lords Proprietors of* CAROLINA. *

CHARLES the Second, by the grace of God king of England, Scotland, France and Ireland, Defender of the Faith, &c. To all to whom these presents shall come, greeting.

I. Whereas our right trusty and right well beloved cousins and counsellors, Edward earl of Clarendon, our high-chancellor of England, and George duke of Albemarle, master of our horse, and captain general of all our forces, our right trusty and well beloved William lord Craven, John lord Berkley, our right trusty and well beloved councellor Anthony lord Ashley, chancellor of our Exchequer, Sir George Carteret knight and baronet, vice-chamberlain of our household, and our trusty and well beloved Sir William Berkley knight, and Sir John Colleton knight and Baronet, being excited with laudable and pious zeal for the propagation of the christian faith, and the enlargement of our empire and dominions, have humbly besought leave of us, by their industry and charge, to transport and make an ample colony of our subjects, natives of our kingdom of England, and elsewhere within our dominions, unto a certain country hereafter described, in the parts of America, not yet cultivated or planted, and only inhabited by some barbarous people who have no knowledge of Almighty God.

Edward earl of Clarendon, &c. having besought the King for leave to make a colony in America, not yet cultivated or planted.

II. And whereas the said Edward earl of Clarendon, George duke of Albemarle, William lord Craven, John lord Berkley, Anthony lord Ashley, Sir George Carteret, Sir William Berkley, Sir John Colleton, have humbly besought us to give, grant and confirm unto them and their heirs the said

The King gives, grants and confirms unto them all that territory in America, bounded within 36 and 31 degrees northern latitude, and west as far as the south-seas.

* This and the succeeding charter are printed in this collection of papers, in order to be preserved. But they are of no force, having been surrendered to the King in the year 1729, and an act of Parliament passed in the same year, establishing the agreement of surrender: but reserving to Lord Carteret, afterwards Earl Granville, his property, who did not chuse to join in the surrender.

ſaid country, with privileges and juriſdictions requiſite for the good government and ſafety thereof. Know ye therefore, That we favouring the pious and noble purpoſe of the ſaid Edward earl of Clarendon, George duke of Albemarle, William lord Craven, John lord Berkley, Anthony lord Aſhley, Sir George Carteret, Sir William Berkley, and Sir John Colleton, of our ſpecial grace, certain knowledge and meer motion, have given, granted and confirmed, and by this our preſent charter, for us, our heirs and ſucceſſors, do give, grant and confirm unto the ſaid Edward earl of Clarendon, George duke of Albemarle, William lord Craven, John lord Berkley, Anthony lord Aſhley, Sir George Carteret, Sir William Berkley, and Sir John Colleton, their heirs and aſſigns, all that territory or tract of ground, ſituate, lying and being within our dominions of America, extending from the north-end of the iſland called Lucke-iſland, which lieth in the ſouthern Virginia ſeas, and within ſix and thirty degrees of the northern latitude, and to the weſt as far as the ſouth-ſeas, and ſo ſoutherly as far as the river St. Matthias, which bordereth upon the coaſt of Florida, and within one and thirty degrees of northern latitude, and ſo weſt in a direct line as far as the ſouth-ſeas aforeſaid; together with all and ſingular ports, harbours, bays, rivers, iſles and iſlets belonging to the country aforeſaid, and alſo all the ſoil, lands, fields, woods, mountains, fields, lakes, rivers, bays and iſlets, ſituate or being within the bounds or limits aforeſaid, with the fiſhing of all ſorts of fiſh, whales, ſturgeons and all other royal fiſhes in the ſea, bays, iſlets and rivers, within the premiſes, and the fiſh therein taken; and moreover all veins, mines, quarries, as well diſcovered as not diſcovered, of gold, ſilver, gems, precious ſtones, and all other whatſoever, be it of ſtones, metals, or any other thing whatſoever found, or to be found within the countries, iſles and limits aforeſaid.

With the patronage and other juriſdictions and privileges.

III. And furthermore the patronage and avowſons of all the churches and chappels, which as the chriſtian religion ſhall increaſe within the country, iſles, iſlets and limits aforeſaid, ſhall happen hereafter to be erected, together with licence and power to build and found churches, chappels and oratories in convenient and fit places, within the ſaid bounds and limits, and to cauſe them to be dedicated and conſecrated according to the eccleſiaſtical laws of our kingdom of England, together with all and ſingular the like and as ample rights, juriſdictions, priviledges, prerogatives, royalties, liberties, immunities

immunities and franchiſes of what kind ſoever, within the countries, iſles, iſlets and limits aforeſaid.

IV. To have, uſe, exerciſe and enjoy, and in as ample manner as any biſhop of Durham in our kingdom of England ever heretofore have held, uſed or enjoyed, or of right ought or could have, uſe or enjoy. And them the ſaid Edward earl of Clarendon, George duke of Albemarle, William lord Craven, John lord Berkley, Anthony lord Aſhley, Sir George Carteret, Sir William Berkley, and Sir John Colleton, their heirs and aſſigns, we do by theſe preſents for us our heirs and ſucceſſors, make, create, and conſtitute the true and abſolute lords and proprietors of the country aforeſaid, and of all other the premiſes; ſaving always the faith, allegiance and ſovereign dominion due to us, our heirs and ſucceſſors for the ſame, and ſaving alſo the right, title, and intereſt of all and every our ſubjects of the Engliſh nation, which are now planted within the limits and bounds aforeſaid, (if any be). To have, hold, poſſeſs and enjoy the ſaid country, iſles, iſlets, and all and ſingular other the premiſes to them the ſaid Edward earl of Clarendon, George duke of Albemarle, William lord Craven, John lord Berkeley, Anthony lord Aſhley, Sir George Carteret, Sir William Berkley, and Sir John Colleton, their heirs and aſſigns for ever, to be holden of us, our heirs and ſucceſſors, as of our manor of Eaſt Greenwich in our county of Kent, in free and common ſoccage, and not in capite, nor by knights ſervice; yielding and paying yearly to us, our heirs and ſucceſſors, for the ſame, the yearly rent of twenty marks of lawful money of England, at the feaſt of All Saints, yearly for ever; the firſt payment thereof to begin and to be made on the feaſt of All Saints, which ſhall be in the year of our Lord one thouſand ſix hundred and ſixty five, and alſo the fourth part of all gold and ſilver ore, which, within the limits aforeſaid, ſhall from time to time happen to be found.

Creating them the true and abſolute lords and proprietors of the ſaid province.

V. And that the country, thus by us granted and deſcribed, may be dignified by us with as large titles and privileges as any other part of our dominions and territories in that region, know ye that we of our further grace, certain knowledge and mere motion, have thought fit to erect the ſame tract of ground, country and iſland into a province, and out of the fulneſs of our royal power and prerogative, we do for us, our heirs and ſucceſſors, erect, incorporate and ordain the ſame into a province, and do call it the province of Carolina, and ſo from henceforth will have it called; And foraſmuch as we have hereby made

The ſaid tract of ground, country and iſlands erected into a province, by the name of the province of Carolina.

and ordained the aforesaid Edward earl of Clarendon, George duke of Albemarle, William lord Craven, John lord Berkeley, Anthony lord Ashley, Sir George Carterett, Sir William Berkeley, and Sir John Colleton, their heirs and assigns the true lords and proprietors of all the province aforesaid: Know ye therefore moreover, that we, reposing especial trust and confidence in their fidelity, wisdom, justice, and provident circumspection, for us, our heirs and successors, do grant full and absolute power, by virtue of these presents, to them the said Edward earl of Clarendon, George duke of Albemarle, William lord Craven, John lord Berkeley Anthony lord Ashley, Sir George Carterett, Sir William Berkeley, and Sir John Colleton, and their heirs, for the good and happy government of the said province, to ordain, make, enact, and under their seals to publish any laws whatsoever, either appertaining to the public state of the said province, or to the private utility of particular persons, according to their best descretion, of and with the advice, assent and approbation of the freemen of the said province, or of the greater part of them, or of their delegates or deputies, whom for enacting of the said laws, when and as often as need shall require, we will that the said Edward earl of Clarendon, George duke of Albemarle, William lord Craven, John lord Berkley, Anthony lord Ashley, Sir George Carteret, Sir William Berkley, and Sir John Colleton, and their heirs, shall from time to time assemble, in such manner and form as to them shall seem best, and the same laws duly to execute, upon all people within the said province and limits thereof, for the time being, or which shall be constituted under the power and government of them, or any of them, either sailing towards the said province of Carolina, or returning from thence towards England, or any other of our, or foreign dominions, by imposition of penalties, imprisonment, or any other punishment; yea, if it shall be needful, and the quality of the offence requires it, by taking away member and life, either by them the said Edward earl of Clarendon, George duke of Albemarle, William lord Craven, John lord Berkley, Anthony lord Ashley, Sir George Carteret, Sir William Berkley, and Sir John Colleton, and their heirs, or by them, or their deputies, lieutenants, judges, justices, magistrates, officers, and ministers, to be ordained or appointed, according to the tenor and true intention of these presents; and likewise to appoint and establish any judges or justices, magistrates

The King grants power to ordain and enact laws for the whole province or any particular person thereof.

magiſtrates or officers whatſoever, within the ſaid province, at ſea or land, in ſuch manner and form, as unto the ſaid Edward earl of Clarendon, George duke of Albemarle, William lord Craven, John lord Berkley, Anthony lord Aſhley, Sir George Carteret, Sir William Berkley, and Sir John Colleton, and their heirs, ſhall ſeem moſt convenient: Alſo to remit, releaſe, pardon, and aboliſh, (whether before judgment or after) all crimes and offences whatſoever, againſt the ſaid laws, and to do all and every other thing and things, which unto the compleat eſtabliſhment of juſtice unto courts, ſeſſions and forms of judicature, and manners of proceedings therein, do belong, although in theſe preſents, expreſs mention be not made thereof; and by judges, by him or them delegated, to award, proceſs, hold pleas, and determine in all the ſaid courts, and places of judicature, all actions, ſuits, and cauſes whatſoever, as well criminal as civil, real, mixt, perſonal, or of any other kind or nature whatſoever; which laws, ſo as aforeſaid to be publiſhed, our pleaſure is, and we do require, enjoin and command, ſhall be abſolute, firm and available in law, and that all the liege people of us, our heirs and ſucceſſors, within the ſaid province of Carolina, do obſerve and keep the ſame inviolably, in thoſe parts, ſo far as they concern them, under the pains and penalties therein expreſſed, or to be expreſſed; provided nevertheleſs, that the ſaid laws be conſonant to reaſon, and as near as may be conveniently, agreeable to the laws and cuſtoms of this our kingdom of England.

And to appoint any judges or juſtices, magiſtrates or officers whatſoever.

VI. And becauſe ſuch aſſemblies of freeholders, cannot be ſo conveniently called, as there may be occaſion to require the ſame; we do therefore by theſe preſents, give and grant unto the ſaid Edward earl of Clarendon, George duke of Albemarle, William lord Craven, John lord Berkley, Anthony lord Aſhley, Sir George Carteret, Sir William Berkley, and Sir John Colleton, their heirs and aſſigns, by themſelves or their magiſtrates, in that behalf lawfully authorized, full power and authority, from time to time, to make and ordain fit and wholeſome orders and ordinances, within the province aforeſaid, to be kept and obſerved, as well for the keeping of the peace, as for the better government of the people there abiding, and to publiſh the ſame to all to whom it may concern; which ordinances, we do by theſe preſents, ſtreightly charge and command to be inviolably obſerved, within the ſaid province,

And till aſſemblies of freeholders can be called,

The ſaid lords proprietors impowered to make orders and ordinances.

vince, under the penalties therein expreſſed, ſo as ſuch ordinances be reaſonable, and not repugnant or contrary, but as near as may be, agreeable to the laws and ſtatutes of this our kingdom of England, and ſo as the ſame ordinances do not extend to the binding, charging, or taking away, of the right or intereſt, of any perſon or perſons, in their freehold, goods or chattels, whatſoever.

Licence given to all the King's liege people to tranſport themſelves to the ſaid province.

VII. And to the end the ſaid province may be the more happily encreaſed, by the multitude of people reſorting thither, and may likewiſe be the more ſtrongly defended from the incurſions of ſavages, and other enemies, pirates and robbers, therefore we, for us, our heirs and ſucceſſors, do give and grant by theſe preſents, power, licence, and liberty, unto all the liege people, of us, our heirs and ſucceſſors, in our kingdom of England, or elſewhere, within any other our dominions, iſlands, colonies, or plantations, (excepting thoſe who ſhall be eſpecially forbidden) to tranſport themſelves and families unto the ſaid province, with convenient ſhipping and fitting proviſions, and there to ſettle themſelves, dwell, and inhabit, any law, ſtatute, act, ordinance or other thing to the contrary, in any wiſe, notwithſtanding. And we will alſo, and of our more ſpecial grace, for us, our heirs and ſucceſſors, do ſtreightly enjoin, ordain, conſtitute and command, that the ſaid province of Carolina, ſhall be of our allegiance, and that all and ſingular the ſubjects and liege people of us, our heirs and ſucceſſors, tranſported, or to be tranſported into the ſaid province, and the children of them, and of ſuch as ſhall deſcend from them, there born, or hereafter to be born, be and ſhall be, denizons and lieges of us, our heirs and ſucceſſors, of this our kingdom of England, and be in all things held, treated and reputed as the liege faithful people of us, our heirs and ſucceſſors, born within this our ſaid kingdom, or any other of our dominions, and may inherit, or otherwiſe purchaſe and receive, take, hold, buy, and poſſeſs any lands, tenements or hereditaments within the ſame places, and them may occupy, poſſeſs and enjoy, give, ſell, aliene and bequeathe; as likewiſe all liberties, franchiſes and privileges of this our kingdom of England, and of other our dominions aforeſaid, and may freely and quietly, have, poſſeſs and enjoy, as our liege people born within the ſame, without the leaſt moleſtation, vexation, trouble or grievance, of us, our heirs and ſucceſſors, any ſtatute, act, ordinance or proviſion to the contrary notwithſtanding.

VIII. And furthermore, that our subjects of this our said kingdom of England, and other our dominions, may be the rather encouraged to undertake this expedition, with ready and chearful minds; know ye, that we, of our special grace, certain knowledge and mere motion, do give and grant by vertue of these presents, as well to the said Edward earl of Clarendon, George duke of Albemarle, William lord Craven, John lord Berkley, Anthony lord Ashley, Sir George Carteret, Sir William Berkley, and Sir John Colleton, and their heirs, as unto all others as shall from time to time repair unto the said province, with a purpose to inhabit there, or to trade with the natives of the said province, full liberty and licence to lade and freight in any port whatsoever, of us, our heirs and successors, and into the said province of Carolina, by them, their servants and assigns, to transport all and singular their goods, wares and merchandizes; as likewise all sorts of grain whatsoever, and any other things whatsoever, necessary for food and cloathing, not prohibited by the laws and statutes of our kingdoms and dominions to be carried out of the same, without any let or molestation, of us, our heirs and successors, or of any other of our officers or ministers whatsoever, saving also to us, our heirs and successors, the customs and other duties and payments, due for the said wares and merchandizes, according to the several rates of the places from whence they shall be transported. We will also, and by these presents, for us, our heirs and successors, do give and grant licence by this our charter, unto the said Edward earl of Clarendon, George duke of Albemarle, William lord Craven, John lord Berkley, Anthony lord Ashley, Sir George Carteret, Sir William Berkley, and Sir John Colleton, their heirs and assigns, and to all the inhabitants and dwellers in the province aforesaid, both present and to come, full power and absolute authority, to import or unlade, by themselves, or their servants, factors or assigns, all merchandizes and goods whatsoever, that shall arise of the fruits and commodities of the said province, either by land or by sea, into any of the ports of us, our heirs and successors, in our kingdom of England, Scotland or Ireland, or otherwise to dispose of the same goods, in the said ports; and if need be, within one year next after the unlading, to lade the said merchandizes and goods again into the same, or other ships, and to export the same into any other countries, either of our dominions or foreign, being in amity with us, our heirs and successors,

The King grants licence to freight in every port, and to transport goods, wares and merchandizes, &c. saving to the King the customs and duties.

successors, so as they pay such customs, subsidies and other duties for the same, to us, our heirs and successors, as the rest of our subjects of this our kingdom, for the time being, shall be bound to pay, beyond which we will not that the inhabitants of the said province of Carolina, shall be any ways charged.

Sundry goods to be imported & exported custom free.

IX. Provided nevertheless, and our will and pleasure is, and we have further, for the consideration aforesaid, of our more especial grace, certain knowledge and meer motion, given and granted, and by these presents, for us, our heirs and successors, do give and grant unto the said Edward earl of Clarendon, George duke of Albemarle, William lord Craven, John lord Berkley, Anthony lord Ashley, Sir George Carteret, Sir William Berkley, and Sir John Colleton, their heirs and assigns, full and free licence, liberty and authority, at any time or times, from and after the feast of St Michael the arch-angel, which shall be in the year of our Lord Christ one thousand six hundred sixty and seven, as well to import, and bring into any of our dominions, from the said province of Carolina, or any part thereof, the several goods and commodities herein after mentioned, that is to say, silks, wine, currants, raisins, capers, wax, almonds, oyl and olives, without paying or answering, unto us, our heirs or successors, any custom, import, or other duty, for, or in respect thereof, for and during the term and space of seven years, to commence and be accompted, from and after the first importation of four tuns of any of the said goods, in any one bottom, ship or vessel from the said province, into any of our dominions; as also to export and carry out of any of our dominions into the said province of Carolina, custom free, all sorts of tools, which shall be useful or necessary for the planters there, in the accommodation and improvement of the premises, any thing before, in these presents contained, or any law, act, statute, prohibition, or other matter, or any thing heretofore had, made, enacted or provided, or hereafter to be had, made, enacted or provided to the contrary, in any wise notwithstanding.

Ports, harbours, &c. to be constituted.

X. And furthermore, of our more ample and especial grace, certain knowledge, and meer motion, we do, for us, our heirs and successors, grant unto the said Edward earl of Clarendon, George duke of Albemarle, William lord Craven, John lord Berkley, Anthony lord Ashley, Sir George Carteret, Sir William Berkley, and Sir John Colleton, their heirs

heirs and aſſigns, full and obſolute power and authority, to make, erect and conſtitute, within the ſaid province of Carolina, and the iſles and iſlets aforeſaid, ſuch, and ſo many ſea ports, harbours, creeks and other places, for diſcharge and unlading of goods and merchandizes out of ſhips, boats and other veſſels, and for lading of them, in ſuch and ſo many places, and with ſuch juriſdiction, privileges and franchiſes, unto the ſaid ports belonging, as to them ſhall ſeem moſt expedient, and that all and ſingular the ſhips, boats and other veſſels, which ſhall come for merchandizes, and trade into the ſaid province, or ſhall depart out of the ſame, ſhall be laden and unladen at ſuch ports only, as ſhall be erected and conſtituted by the ſaid Edward earl of Clarendon, George duke of Albemarle, William lord Craven, John lord Berkley, Anthony lord Aſhley, Sir George Carteret, Sir William Berkeley, and Sir John Colleton, their heirs and aſſigns, and not elſe where, any uſe, cuſtom, or any other thing to the contrary in any wiſe notwithſtanding.

The ſubſidies to belong to the lords proprietors.

XI. And we do furthermore will, appoint and ordain, by theſe preſents for us, our heirs and ſucceſſors, do grant unto the ſaid Edward earl of Clarendon, George duke of Albemarle, William lord Craven, John lord Berkeley, Anthony lord Aſhley, Sir George Carteret, Sir William Berkeley, and Sir John Colleton, their heirs and aſſigns, that they the ſaid Edward earl of Clarendon, George duke of Albemarle, William lord Craven, John lord Berkeley, Anthony lord Aſhley, Sir George Carteret, Sir William Berkely, and Sir John Colleton, their heirs and aſſigns, may from time to time for ever, have and enjoy, the cuſtoms and ſubſidies in the ports, harbours, creeks and other places within the province aforeſaid, payable for goods, merchandize and wares there laded, or to be laded or unladed, the ſaid cuſtoms to be reaſonably aſſeſſed, upon any occaſion, by themſelves, and by and with the conſent of the free people there, or the greater part of them as aforeſaid; to whom we give power, by theſe preſents, for us our heirs and ſucceſſors, upon juſt cauſe, and in a due proportion to aſſeſs and impoſe the ſame.

The lords proprietors may aſſign and grant the premiſes or any part thereof

XII. And further, of our ſpecial grace, certain knowledge, and mere motion, we have given, granted and confirmed, and by theſe preſents, for us, our heirs and ſucceſſors, do give, grant and confirm unto the ſaid Edward earl of Clarendon, George duke of Albemarle, William lord Craven, John lord Berkely, Anthony lord Aſhley, Sir George

Carteret,

to him or them that will purchase the same.

Carteret, Sir William Berkley and Sir John Colleton, their heirs and aſſigns, full and abſolute licence, power and authority, that the ſaid Edward earl of Clarendon, George duke of Albemarle, William Lord Craven, John lord Berkeley, Anthony lord Aſhley, Sir George Carteret, Sir William Berkley, and Sir John Colleton, their heirs and aſſigns, from time to time hereafter for ever, at his and their will and pleaſure, may aſſign, alien, grant, demiſe or enfeof the premiſes, or any parte or parcels thereof, to him or them that ſhall be willing to purchaſe the ſame, and to ſuch perſon or perſons as they ſhall think fit, to have and to hold, to them the ſaid perſon or perſons, their heirs and aſſigns, in fee ſimple or fee tayle, or for term of life, or lives, or years, to be held of them the ſaid Edward earl of Clarendon, George duke of Albemarle, William lord Craven, John lord Berkley, Anthony lord Aſhley, Sir George Carteret, Sir William Berkley, and Sir John Colleton, their heirs and aſſigns, by ſuch rents, ſervices and cuſtoms, as ſhall ſeem meet to the ſaid Edward earl of Clarendon, George duke of Albemarle, William lord Craven, John lord Berkley, Anthony lord Aſhley, Sir George Carteret, Sir William Berkley, and Sir John Colleton, their heirs and aſſigns, and not immediately of us, our heirs and ſucceſſors, and to the ſame perſon and perſons, and to all and every of them, we do give and grant by theſe, preſents, for us, our heirs and ſucceſſors, licence authority and power, that ſuch perſon or perſons, may have or take the premiſes, or any parcel thereof, of the ſaid Edward earl of Clarendon, George duke of Albemarle, William lord Craven, John lord Berkley, Anthony lord Aſhley, Sir George Carteret, Sir William Berkley, and Sir John Colleton, their heirs and aſſigns, and the ſame to hold, to themſelves, their heirs or aſſigns, in what eſtate of inheritance whatſoever, in fee ſimple or fee tayle, or otherwiſe, as to them and the ſaid Edward earl of Clarendon, George duke of Albemarle, William lord Craven, John lord Berkeley, Anthony lord Aſhley, Sir George Carteret, Sir William Berkley, and Sir John Colleton, their heirs and aſſigns, ſhall ſeem expedient; the ſtatute made in the parliament of Edward, ſon of King Henry, heretofore King of England, our predeceſſor, commonly called the ſtatute of *Quia emptores terrarum*; or any other ſtatute, act, ordinance, uſe, law, cuſtom or any other matter, cauſe or thing heretofore publiſhed or provided to the contrary, in any wiſe, notwithſtanding.

XIII. And

XIII. And becauſe many perſons born or inhabiting in the ſaid province, for their deſerts and ſervices, may expect and be capable of marks of honour and favour, which, in reſpect of the great diſtance, cannot be conveniently conferred by us; our will and pleaſure therefore is, and we do by theſe preſents give and grant unto the ſaid Edward earl of Clarendon, George duke of Albemarle, William lord Craven, John lord Berkley, Anthony lord Aſhley, Sir George Carteret, Sir William Berkley, and Sir John Colleton, their heirs and aſſigns, full power and authority, to give and confer, unto and upon, ſuch of the inhabitants of the ſaid province, as they ſhall think do, or ſhall merit the ſame, ſuch marks of favour and titles of honour, as they ſhall think fit, ſo as theſe titles of honour be not the ſame as are enjoyed by, or conferred upon, any of the ſubjects of this our kingdom of England.

The lords proprietors impowered to confer titles of honour.

XIV. And further alſo, we do by theſe preſents, for us, our heirs and ſucceſſors, give and grant licence to them the ſaid Edward earl of Clarendon, George duke of Albemarle, William lord Craven, John lord Berkley, Anthony lord Aſhley, Sir George Carteret, Sir William Berkley, and Sir John Colleton, their heirs and aſſigns, full power, liberty and licence to erect, raiſe and build, within the ſaid province and places aforeſaid, or any part or parts thereof, ſuch, and ſo many forts, fortreſſes, caſtles, cities, burroughs, towns, villages and other fortifications whatſoever, and the ſame, or any of them to fortify and furniſh with ordnance, powder, ſhot, armory and all other weapons, ammunition, habilements of war, both offenſive and defenſive, as ſhall be thought fit and convenient for the ſafety and welfare of the ſaid province and places, or any part thereof, and the ſame, or any of them, from time to time, as occaſion ſhall require, to diſmantle, disfurniſh, demoliſh and pull down, and alſo to place, conſtitute and appoint, in and over all or any of the ſaid caſtles, forts, fortifications, cities, towns and places aforeſaid, governors, deputy governors, magiſtrates, ſheriffs and other officers, civil and military, as to them ſhall ſeem meet, and to the ſaid cities, burroughs, towns, villages, or any other place or places within the ſaid province, to grant letters or charters of incorporation, with all liberties, franchiſes and privileges requiſite and uſeful, or to, or within any corporations within this our kingdom of England, granted or belonging; and in the ſame cities, burroughs, towns and other places, to conſtitute, erect and appoint, ſuch, and

And to erect forts, caſtles, cities, towns and other fortifications.

I ſo

ſo many markets, marts and fairs, as ſhall in that behalf be thought fit and neceſſary, and further alſo to erect and make in the province aforeſaid, or any part thereof, ſo many mannors, as to them ſhall ſeem meet and convenient, and in every of the ſame mannors, to have and to hold a court baron, with all things whatſoever which to a court baron do belong, and to have and to hold views of frank pledge and court leet, for the conſervation of the peace, and better government of thoſe parts, within ſuch limits, juriſdictions and precincts, as by the ſaid Edward earl of Clarendon, George duke of Albemarle, William lord Craven, John lord Berkley, Anthony lord Aſhley, Sir George Carteret, Sir William Berkley, and Sir John Colleton, or their heirs, ſhall be appointed for that purpoſe, with all things whatſoever, which to a court leet or view of frank pledge do belong, the ſaid court to be holden by ſtewards, to be deputed and authorized by the ſaid Edward earl of Clarendon, George duke of Albemarle, William lord Craven, John lord Berkley, Anthony lord Aſhley, Sir George Carteret, Sir William Berkley, and Sir John Colleton, or their heirs, or by the lords of other mannors and leets for the time being, when the ſame ſhall be erected.

Power to levy, muſter and train men, and make war.

XV. And becauſe that in ſo remote a country, and ſcituate among ſo many barbarous nations, and the invaſions as well of ſalvages as other enemies, pirates and robbers, may probably be feared; therefore we have given, and for us our heirs and ſucceſſors, do give power by theſe preſents, unto the ſaid Edward earl of Clarendon, George duke of Albemarle, William lord Craven, John lord Berkley, Anthony lord Aſhley, Sir George Carteret, Sir William Berkley, and Sir John Colleton, their heirs and aſſigns, by themſelves, or their captains, or other their officers, to levy, muſter and train, all ſorts of men, of what condition, or whereſoever born, in the ſaid province, for the time being; and to make war, and purſue the enemies aforeſaid, as well by ſea as by land, ; yea, even without the limits of the ſaid province, and by God's aſſiſtance, to vanquiſh and take them, and being taken, to put them to death by the law of war, or to ſave them at their pleaſure; and to do all and every other thing, which unto the charge of a captain general of an army belongeth, or hath accuſtomed to belong, as fully and freely as any captain general of an army hath or ever had the ſame.

XVI. Alſo

XVI. Alſo, our will and pleaſure is, and by this our charter we give unto the ſaid Edward earl of Clarendon, George duke of Albemarle, William lord Craven, John lord Berkley, Anthony lord Aſhley, Sir George Carteret, Sir William Berkley and Sir John Colleton, their heirs and aſſigns, full power, liberty, and authority, in caſe of rebellion, tumult or ſedition, (if any ſhould happen) which God forbid, either upon the land within the province aforeſaid, or upon the main ſea, in making a voyage thither, or returning from thence, by him and themſelves, their captains, deputies and officers, to be authorized under his or their ſeals for that purpoſe. To whom alſo, for us, our heirs and ſucceſſors, we do give and grant, by theſe preſents, full power and authority, to exerciſe martial law againſt mutinous and ſeditious perſons of thoſe parts, ſuch as ſhall refuſe to ſubmit themſelves to their government, or ſhall refuſe to ſerve in the wars, or ſhall fly to the enemy, or forſake their colours or enſigns, or be loyterers or ſtragglers, or otherwiſe howſoever offending againſt law, cuſtom or diſcipline military, as freely and in as ample manner and form as any captain general of an army, by virtue of his office, might or hath accuſtomed to uſe the ſame.

And to exerciſe martial law.

XVII. And our further pleaſure is, and by theſe preſents, for us, our heirs and ſucceſſors, we do grant unto the ſaid Edward earl of Clarendon, George duke of Albemarle, William lord Craven, John lord Berkley, Anthony lord Aſhley, Sir George Carteret, Sir William Berkley, and Sir John Colleton, their heirs and aſſigns, and to all the tenants and inhabitants of the ſaid province of Carolina, both preſent and to come, and to every of them, that the ſaid province, and the tenants and inhabitants thereof, ſhall not, from henceforth, be held or reputed a member or part of any colony whatſoever in America, or elſewhere, now tranſported or made, or hereafter to be tranſported or made; nor ſhall be depending on, or ſubject to their government, in any thing, but be abſolutely ſeparated and divided from the ſame: and our pleaſure is, by theſe preſents, that they be ſeparated, and that they be ſubject immediately to our crown of England, as depending thereof for ever; and that the inhabitants of the ſaid province, nor any of them, ſhall at any time hereafter be compelled, or compellable, or be any ways ſubject or liable, to appear or anſwer to any matter, ſuit, cauſe or plaint whatſoever, out of the province aforeſaid, in any other of our iſlands, colonies or dominions in

The province of Carolina & the inhabitants thereof to be ſubject immediately to the crown of England.

America, or elſewhere, other than in our realm of England and dominion of Wales.

The lords proprietors impowered to grant liberty of conſcience.

XVIII. And becauſe it may happen, that ſome of the people and inhabitants of the ſaid province, cannot in their private opinions conform to the public exerciſe of religion, according to the liturgy, form and ceremonies of the church of England, or take and ſubſcribe the oaths and articles made and eſtabliſhed in that behalf, and for that the ſame, by reaſon of the remote diſtances of theſe places, will, we hope, be no breach of the unity and uniformity eſtabliſhed in this nation, our will and pleaſure therefore is, and we do by theſe preſents, for us, our heirs and ſucceſſors, give and grant unto the ſaid Edward earl of Clarendon, George duke of Albemarle, William lord Craven, John lord Berkley, Anthony lord Aſhley, Sir George Carteret, Sir William Berkley, and Sir John Colleton, their heirs and aſſigns, full and free licence, liberty and authority, by ſuch legal ways and means as they ſhall think fit, to give and grant unto ſuch perſon and perſons inhabiting and being within the ſaid province, or any part thereof, who really in their judgments, and for conſcience ſake, cannot or ſhall not conform to the ſaid liturgy and ceremonies, and take and ſubſcribe the oaths and articles aforeſaid, or any of them, ſuch indulgencies and diſpenſations in that behalf, for and during ſuch time and times, and with ſuch limitations and reſtrictions, as they the ſaid Edward earl of Clarendon, George duke of Albemarle, William lord Craven, John lord Berkley, Anthony lord Aſhley, Sir John Carteret, Sir William Berkley, and Sir John Colleton, their heirs or aſſigns, ſhall in their diſcretion think fit and reaſonable; and with this expreſs proviſo and limitation alſo, that ſuch perſon or perſons, to whom ſuch indulgences and diſpenſations ſhall be granted as aforeſaid, do and ſhall, from time to time, declare and continue all fidelity, loyalty and obedience to us, our heirs and ſucceſſors, and be ſubject and obedient to all other the laws, ordinances and conſtitutions of the ſaid province, in all matters whatſoever, as well eccleſiaſtical as civil, and do not in any wiſe diſturb the peace and ſafety thereof, or ſcandalize or reproach the ſaid liturgy, forms and ceremonies, or any thing relating thereunto, or any perſon or perſons whatſoever, for or in reſpect of his or their uſe or exerciſe thereof, or his or their obedience or conformity thereunto.

XIX. And in caſe it ſhall happen, that any doubts or queſtions ſhould ariſe, concerning the true ſenſe and underſtanding

derstanding of any word, clause or sentence, contained in this our present charter, we will, ordain, and command, that at all times, and in all things, such interpretation be made thereof, and allowed in all and every of our courts whatsoever, as lawfully may be adjudged most advantageous and favourable to the said Edward earl of Clarendon, George duke of Albemarle, William lord Craven, John lord Berkley, Anthony lord Ashley, Sir George Carteret, Sir William Berkley, and Sir John Colleton, their heirs and assigns, although express mention be not made in these presents, of the true yearly value and certainty of the premises, or any part thereof, or of any other gifts and grants made by us, our ancestors or predecessors, to them the said Edward earl of Clarendon, George duke of Albemarle, William lord Craven, John lord Berkley, Anthony lord Ashley, Sir George Carteret, Sir William Berkley, and Sir John Colleton, or any other person or persons whatsoever, or any statute, act, ordinance, provision, proclamation or restraint heretofore had, made, published, ordained or provided, or any other thing, cause or matter whatsoever, to the contrary thereof, in any wise notwithstanding.

In case of doubts or questions, the interpretation to be made most advantageous and favourable to the lords proprietors.

In witness, &c. Witness the King, at Westminster, the four and twentieth day of March, in the fifteenth year of our reign.

Per ipsum regem.

The second Charter, granted by King Charles II. *to the Lords Proprietors of* CAROLINA.

His Majesty King Charles II.

CHARLES the Second, by the grace of God king of England, Scotland, France and Ireland, Defender of the Faith, &c.

Reciting a former charter, wherein was granted to Edward earl of Clarendon, &c. all that territory in America called Carolina.

I. Whereas by our letters patents, bearing date the four and twentieth day of March, in the fifteenth year of our reign, we were graciously pleased to grant unto our right trusty and right well beloved cousin and counsellor Edward earl of Clarendon, our high-chancellor of England, our right trusty and right intirely beloved cousin and councellor George duke of Albemarle, master of our horse, our right trusty and well beloved William now earl of Craven, our right trusty and well beloved councellor John lord Berkley, our right trusty and well beloved councellor Anthony lord Ashley, chancellor of our Exchequer, our right trusty and well beloved councellor Sir George Carteret knight and baronet, vice-chamberlain of our houshold, our right trusty and well beloved Sir John Colleton, knight and baronet, and Sir William Berkley knight, all that province, territory or tract of ground, called Carolina, situate, lying and being within our dominions of America, extending from the north-end of the island called Lucke-island, which lieth in the southern Virginia seas, and within six and thirty degrees of the northern latitude, and to the west as far as the south-seas, and so respectively as far as the river of Matthias, which bordereth upon the coast of Florida, and within one and thirty degrees of the northern latitude, and so west in a direct line as far as the south-seas aforesaid.

His said Majesty is now pleased to enlarge the said grant unto the said lords proprietors.

II. Know ye, that we, at the humble request of the said grantees in the aforesaid letters patents named, and as a further mark of our especial favour towards them, we are graciously pleased to enlarge our said grant unto them, according to the bounds and limits hereafter specified, and in favour to the pious and noble purpose of the said Edward earl of Clarendon, George duke of Albemarle, William earl of Craven, John lord Berkley, Anthony lord Ashley, Sir George Carteret, Sir John Colleton, and Sir William Berkley, their heirs and assigns, all that province, territory or tract of ground

ground, ſcituate, lying and being within our dominions of America aforeſaid, extending north and eaſtward as far as the north end of Charahake river, or gulet, upon a ſtreight weſterly line to Wyonoake creek, which lies within or about the degrees of thirty-ſix and thirty minutes northern latitude, and ſo weſt in a direct line as far as the ſouth-ſeas; and ſouth and weſtward as far as the degrees of twenty-nine incluſive northern latitude, and ſo weſt in a direct line as far as the ſouth-ſeas; together with all and ſingular ports, harbours, bays, rivers and iſlets belonging unto the province or territory aforeſaid, and alſo all the ſoil, lands, fields, woods, mountains, ferms, lakes, rivers, bays and iſlets, ſcituate, or being within the bounds or limits laſt before mentioned; with the fiſhing of all ſorts of fiſh, whales, ſturgeons, and all other royal fiſhes in the ſea, bays, iſlets and rivers within the premiſes, and the fiſh therein taken, together with the royalty of the ſea upon the coaſts within the limits aforeſaid. And moreover all veins, mines and quarries, as well diſcovered as not diſcovered, of gold, ſilver, gems and precious ſtones, and all other whatſoever, be it of ſtones, metal or any other thing found, or to be found within the province, territory, iſlets and limits aforeſaid.

III. And furthermore the patronage and avowſons of all the churches and chapels, which, as chriſtian religion ſhall increaſe within the province, territory, iſlets and limits aforeſaid, ſhall happen hereafter to be erected; together with licence and power to build and found churches, chapels and oratories in convenient and fit places within the ſaid bounds and limits, and to cauſe them to be dedicated and conſecrated, according to the eccleſiaſtical laws of our kingdom of England; together with all and ſingular the like, and as ample rights, juriſdictions, privileges, prerogatives, royalties, liberties, immunities and franchiſes of what kind ſoever, within the countries, iſles, iſlets and limits aforeſaid. To have, hold, uſe, exerciſe and enjoy the ſame, as amply, fully, and in as ample manner as any biſhop of Durham in our kingdom of England ever heretofore had, held, uſed or enjoyed, or of right ought or could have, uſe or enjoy. And them the ſaid Edward earl of Clarendon, George duke of Albemarle, William earl of Craven, John lord Berkley, Anthony lord Aſhley, Sir George Carteret, Sir John Colleton, and Sir William Berkley, their heirs and aſſigns, we do by theſe preſents for us our heirs and ſucceſſors, make, create, and conſtitute the true and abſolute lords and proprietors

With the patronage and avowſons of all churches and chapels.

prietors of the ſaid province or territory, and of all other the premiſes; ſaving always the faith, allegiance and ſovereign dominion due to us, our heirs and ſucceſſors for the ſame: To have, hold, poſſeſs and enjoy the ſaid province, territory, iſlets, and all and ſingular other the premiſes to them the ſaid Edward earl of Clarendon, George duke of Albemarle, William earl of Craven, John lord Berkeley, Anthony lord Aſhley, Sir George Carteret, Sir John Colleton, and Sir William Berkley, their heirs and aſſigns for ever, to be holden of us, our heirs and ſucceſſors, as of our mannor of Eaſt Greenwich in Kent, in free and common ſoccage, and not in capite, or by knights ſervice; yielding and paying yearly to us, our heirs and ſucceſſors, for the ſame, the fourth part of all gold and ſilver ore, which, within the limits hereby granted, ſhall from time to time happen to be found, over and beſides the yearly rent of twenty marks and the fourth part of the gold and ſilver ore, in and by the ſaid recited letters patents reſerved and payable.

The tract of ground hereby granted annexed to the province of Carolina.

IV. And that the province or territory hereby granted and deſcribed, may be dignified with as large titles and priviledges as any other parts of our dominions and territories in that region: Know ye, that we, of our further grace, certain knowledge and mere motion, have thought fit to annex the ſame tract of ground and territory unto the ſame province of Carolina; and out of the fullneſs of our royal power and prerogative, we do for us, our heirs and ſucceſſors, annex and unite the ſame to the ſaid province of Carolina. And foraſmuch as we have made and ordained the aforeſaid Edward earl of Clarendon, George duke of Albemarle, William earl of Craven, John lord Berkeley, Anthony lord Aſhley, Sir George Carterett, Sir John Colleton, and Sir William Berkeley, their heirs and aſſigns, the true lords and proprietors of all the province or territory aforeſaid: Know ye therefore moreover, that we, repoſing eſpecial truſt and confidence in their fidelity, wiſdom, juſtice, and provident circumſpection, for us, our heirs and ſucceſſors, do grant full and abſolute power, by virtue of theſe preſents, to them the ſaid Edward earl of Clarendon, George duke of Albemarle, William earl of Craven, John lord Berkeley Anthony lord Aſhley, Sir George Carterett, Sir John Colleton, Sir William Berkeley, and their heirs and aſſigns, for the good and happy government of the ſaid whole province or territory, full power and authority, to erect, conſtitute and

make

make several counties, baronies and colonies of and within the said provinces, territories, lands and hereditaments, in and by the said recited letters patents and these presents granted, or mentioned to be granted as aforesaid, with several and distinct jurisdictions, powers, liberties and privileges: and also to ordain, make, and enact, and under their seals to publish, any laws and constitutions whatsoever, either appertaining to the public state of the said whole province or territory, or of any distinct or particular county, barony or colony, of or within the same, or to the private utility of particular persons, according to their best discretion, by and with the advice, assent and approbation of the freemen of the said province, or territory, or of the freemen of the county, barony or colony, for which such law or constitution shall be made, or the greater part of them, or of their delegates or deputies, whom for enacting of the said laws, when and as often as need shall require, we will that the said Edward earl of Clarendon, George duke of Albemarle, William earl of Craven, John lord Berkley, Anthony lord Ashley, Sir George Carteret, Sir John Colleton, and Sir William Berkley, and their heirs and assigns, shall from time to time assemble, in such manner and form as to them shall seem best, and the same laws duly to execute, upon all people within the said province or territory, county, barony or colony, and the limits thereof, for the time being, which shall be constituted under the power and government of them, or any of them, either sailing towards the said province or territory of Carolina, or returning from thence towards England, or any other of our, or foreign dominions, by imposition of penalties, imprisonment, or any other punishment; yea, if it be needful, and the quality of the offence require it, by taking away member and life, either by them the said Edward earl of Clarendon, George duke of Albemarle, William earl of Craven, John lord Berkley, Anthony lord Ashley, Sir George Carteret, Sir John Colleton, and Sir William Berkley, and their heirs, or by them, or their deputies, lieutenants, judges, justices, magistrates, officers, ministers, to be ordained and appointed, according to the true tenor and intention of these presents; And likewise to erect or make any court or courts whatsoever of judicature, or otherwise, as shall be requisite; and to appoint and establish any judges or justices, magistrates or officers whatsoever, as well within the said province, as at sea, in such manner and form as unto the said Edward

The lords proprietors impowered to constitute counties, baronies, and colonies within the said province, and to enact laws and constitutions.

And to erect courts of judicature and to appoint judges, justices, &c.

Edward earl of Clarendon, George duke of Albemarle, William earl of Craven, John lord Berkley, Anthony lord Ashley, Sir George Carteret, Sir John Colleton, and Sir William Berkley, and their heirs, shall seem most convenient: Also to remit, release, pardon, and abolish, (either before judgment or after) all crimes and offences whatsoever, against the said laws, and to do all and every other thing and things, which unto the compleat establishment of justice unto courts, sessions and forms of judicature, and manners of proceedings therein, do belong, although in these presents, express mention is not made thereof; and by judges, by him or them delegated, to award process, hold pleas, and determine in all the said courts, and places of judicature, all actions, suits, and causes whatsoever, as well criminal as civil, real, mixt, personal, or of any other kind or nature whatsoever; which laws, so as aforesaid to be published, our pleasure is, and we do enjoin, require and command, shall be absolutely firm and available in law, and that all the liege people of us, our heirs and successors, within the said province or territory, do observe and keep the same inviolably, in those parts, so far as they concern them, under the pains and penalties therein expressed, or to be expressed; provided nevertheless, that the said laws be consonant to reason, and as near as may be conveniently, agreeable to the laws and customs of this our realm of England.

And to make orders and ordinances.

V. And because such assemblies of freeholders, cannot be so suddenly called, as there may be occasion to require the same; we do therefore by these presents, give and grant unto the said Edward earl of Clarendon, George duke of Albemarle, William earl of Craven, John lord Berkley, Anthony lord Ashley, Sir George Carteret, Sir William Berkley, and Sir John Colleton, their heirs and assigns, by themselves or their magistrates, in that behalf lawfully authorized, full power and authority, from time to time, to make and ordain fit and wholesome orders and ordinances, within the province or territoy aforesaid, or any county, barony or province, of or within the same, to be kept and observed, as well for the keeping of the peace, as for the better government of the people there abiding, as to publish the same to all to whom it may concern; which ordinances, we do by these presents, streightly charge and command to be inviolably observed, within the same province, counties, territories, baronies and provinces, under the

the penalties therein expreſſed, ſo as ſuch ordinances be reaſonable, and not repugnant or contrary, but as near as may be, agreeable to the laws and ſtatutes of this our kingdom of England, and ſo as the ſame ordinances do not extend to the binding, charging, or taking away, of the right or intereſt, of any perſon or perſons, in their freehold, goods or chattels, whatſoever.

Licence given to all the King's liege people to tranſport themſelves thither.

VI. And to the end the ſaid province or territory may be the more happily encreaſed, by the multitude of people reſorting thither, and may likewiſe be more ſtrongly defended from the incurſions of ſavages, and other enemies, pirates and robbers, therefore we, for us, our heirs and ſucceſſors, do give and grant by theſe preſents, power, licence, and liberty, unto all the liege people, of us, our heirs and ſucceſſors, in our kingdom of England, or elſewhere, within any other our dominions, iſlands, colonies, or plantations, (excepting thoſe who ſhall be eſpecially forbidden) to tranſport themſelves and families into the ſaid province or territory, with convenient ſhipping and fitting proviſions, and there to ſettle themſelves, dwell, and inhabit, any law, act, ſtatute, ordinance or other thing to the contrary, in any wiſe, notwithſtanding.

The ſaid province to be of the King's allegiance.

VII. And we will alſo, and of our more ſpecial grace, for us, our heirs and ſucceſſors, do ſtreightly enjoin, ordain, conſtitute and command, that the ſaid province or territory, ſhall be of our allegiance, and that all and ſingular the ſubjects and liege people of us, our heirs and ſucceſſors, tranſported, or to be tranſported into the ſaid province, and the children of them, and ſuch as ſhall deſcend from them, there born, or hereafter to be born, be and ſhall be, denizens and lieges of us, our heirs and ſucceſſors, of this our kingdom of England, and be in all things held, treated and reputed as the liege faithful people of us, our heirs and ſucceſſors, born within this our ſaid kingdom, or any other of our dominions, and may inherit, or otherwiſe purchaſe and receive, take, hold, buy, and poſſeſs, any lands, tenements or hereditaments within the ſaid places, and them may occupy, and enjoy, ſell, alien and bequeathe; as likewiſe all liberties, franchiſes and privileges, of this our kingdom, and of other our dominions aforeſaid, may freely and quietly, have, poſſeſs and enjoy, as our liege people born within the ſame, without the leaſt moleſtation, vexation, trouble or grievance, of us, our heirs and

 ſucceſſors,

ſucceſſors, any act, ſtatute, ordinance, proviſion to the contrary notwithſtanding.

The King grants licence to freight in every port, and to tranſport goods, wares and merchandizes, &c. ſaving to the King the cuſtoms and duties.

VIII. And furthermore, that our ſubjects of this our ſaid kingdom of England, and other our dominions, may be the rather encouraged to undertake this expedition, with ready and chearful minds; know ye, that we, of our eſpecial grace, certain knowledge and mere motion, do give and grant by vertue of theſe preſents, as well to the ſaid Edward earl of Clarendon, George duke of Albemarle, William earl of Craven, John lord Berkley, Anthony lord Aſhley, Sir George Carteret, Sir John Colleton, and Sir William Berkley, and their heirs, as unto all others as ſhall from time to time repair unto the ſaid province or territory, with a purpoſe to inhabit there, or to trade with the natives thereof, full liberty and licence to trade and freight in every port whatſoever, of us, our heirs and ſucceſſors, and into the ſaid province of Carolina, by them, their ſervants and aſſigns, to tranſport all and ſingular their goods, wares and merchandizes; as likewiſe all ſorts of grain whatſoever, and any other thing whatſoever, neceſſary for food and cloathing, not prohibited by the laws and ſtatutes of our kingdoms and dominions to be carried out of the ſame, without any let or moleſtation, of us, our heirs and ſucceſſors, or of any other our officers or miniſters whatſoever, ſaving alſo to us, our heirs and ſucceſſors, the cuſtoms and other duties and payments, due for the ſaid wares and merchandizes, according to the ſeveral rates of the places from whence the ſame ſhall be tranſported.

Sundry goods to be imported & exported cuſtom free.

IX. We will alſo, and by theſe preſents, for us, our heirs and ſucceſſors, do give and grant licence by this our charter, unto the ſaid Edward earl of Clarendon, George duke of Albemarle, William earl of Craven, John lord Berkley, Anthony lord Aſhley, Sir George Carteret, Sir John Colleton, and Sir William Berkley, their heirs and aſſigns, and to all the inhabitants and dwellers in the province or territory aforeſaid, both preſent and to come, full power and abſolute authority, to import or unlade, by themſelves, or their ſervants, factors or aſſigns, all merchandizes and goods whatſoever, that ſhall ariſe of the fruits and commodities of the ſaid province or territory, either by land or ſea, into any the ports of us, our heirs and ſucceſſors, in our kingdom of England, Scotland or Ireland, or otherwiſe to diſpoſe of the ſaid goods, in the ſaid ports; and if need be, within one year next after the unlading, to lade the ſaid merchandizes

chandizes and goods again into the ſame, or other ſhips, and to export the ſame into any other countries, either of our dominions or foreign, being in amity with us, our heirs and ſucceſſors, ſo as they pay ſuch cuſtoms, ſubſidies and other duties for the ſame, to us, our heirs and ſucceſſors, as the reſt of our ſubjects of this our kingdom, for the time being, ſhall be bound to pay, beyond which we will not that the inhabitants of the ſaid province or territory, ſhall be any ways charged. Provided nevertheleſs, and our will and pleaſure is, and we have further, for the conſiderations aforeſaid, of our ſpecial grace, certain knowledge and meer motion, given and granted, and by theſe preſents, for us, our heirs and ſucceſſors, do give and grant unto the ſaid Edward earl of Clarendon, George duke of Albemarle, William earl of Craven, John lord Berkley, Anthony lord Aſhley, Sir George Carteret, Sir John Colleton, and Sir William Berkley, their heirs and aſſigns, full and free licence, liberty, power and authority, at any time or times, from and after the feaſt of St Michael the arch-angel, which ſhall be in the year of our Lord Chriſt one thouſand ſix hundred ſixty and ſeven, as well to import, and bring into any our dominions, from the ſaid province of Carolina, or any part thereof, the ſeveral goods and commodities herein after mentioned, that is to ſay, ſilk, wines, currants, raiſins, capers, wax, almonds, oyl and olives, without paying or anſwering, to us, our heirs or ſucceſſors, any cuſtom, import, or other duty, for, or in reſpect thereof, for and during the time and ſpace of ſeven years, to commence and be accompted, from and after the firſt importation of four tuns of any of the ſaid goods, in any one bottom, ſhip or veſſel from the ſaid province or territory into any of our dominions; as alſo to export and carry out of any of our dominions into the ſaid province or territory, cuſtom free, all ſorts of tools, which ſhall be uſeful and neceſſary for the planters there, in the accommodation and improvement of the premiſes, any thing before, in theſe preſents contained, or any law, act, ſtatute, prohibition, or other matter, or thing heretofore had, made, enacted or provided, or hereafter to be had, made, enacted or provided, in any wiſe notwithſtanding.

Ports, harbours, &c. to be conſtituted.

X. And furthermore, of our more ample and eſpecial grace, certain knowledge, and meer motion, we do, for us, our heirs and ſucceſſors, grant unto the ſaid Edward earl of Clarendon, George duke of Albemarle, William earl of Craven,

ven, John lord Berkley, Anthony lord Ashley, Sir George Carteret, Sir John Colleton, and Sir William Berkley, their heirs and assigns, full and absolute power and authority, to make, erect and constitute, within the said province or territory, and the isles and islets aforesaid, such, and so many sea ports, harbours, creeks and other places, for discharge and unlading of goods and merchandizes out of ships, boats and other vessels, and for lading of them, in such and so many places, and with such jurisdiction, privileges and franchises, unto the said ports belonging, as to them shall seem most expedient, and that all and singular the ships, boats and other vessels, which shall come for merchandizes, and trade into the said province or territory, or shall depart out of the same, shall be laden and unladen at such ports only, as shall be erected and constituted by the said Edward earl of Clarendon, George duke of Albemarle, William earl of Craven, John lord Berkley, Anthony lord Ashley, Sir George Carteret, Sir John Colleton, and Sir William Berkley, their heirs and assigns, and not else where, any use, custom, or any thing to the contrary in any wise notwithstanding.

The subsidies to belong to the lords proprietors.

XI. And we do furthermore will, appoint and ordain, and by these presents for us, our heirs and successors, do grant unto the said Edward earl of Clarendon, George duke of Albemarle, William earl of Craven, John lord Berkley, Anthony lord Ashley, Sir George Carteret, Sir John Colleton, and Sir William Berkley, their heirs and assigns, that they the said Edward earl of Clarendon, George duke of Albemarle, William earl of Craven, John lord Berkley, Anthony lord Ashley, Sir George Carteret, Sir John Colleton, and Sir William Berkely, their heirs and assigns, may from time to time for ever, have and enjoy, the customs and subsidies in the ports, harbours, creeks and other places within the province aforesaid, payable for the goods, merchandizes and wares there laded, or to be laded or unladed, the said customs to be reasonably assessed to, upon any occasion, by themselves, and by and with the consent of the free people, or the greater part of them as aforesaid; to whom we give power, by these presents, for us our heirs and successors, upon just cause, and in a due proportion, to assess and impose the same.

The lords proprietors may assign and grant the premises or any

XII. And further, of our special grace, certain knowledge, and mere motion, we have given, granted and confirmed, and by these presents, for us, our heirs and successors, do give, grant and confirm unto the said Edward earl of Clarendon, George duke of Albemarle, William earl of Craven,

Craven, John lord Berkley, Anthony lord Aſhley, Sir George Carteret, Sir John Colleton, and Sir William Berkley, their heirs and aſſigns, full and abſolute power, licence and authority, that the ſaid Edward earl of Clarendon, George duke of Albemarle, William earl of Craven, John lord Berkley, Anthony lord Aſhley, Sir George Carteret, Sir John Colleton, and Sir William Berkley, their heirs and aſſigns, from time to time hereafter for ever, at his or their will and pleaſure, may aſſign, alien, grant, demiſe or enfeof the premiſes, or any part or parcels thereof, to him or them that ſhall be willing to purchaſe the ſame, and to ſuch perſon or perſons as they ſhall think fit, to have and to hold, to them the ſaid perſon or perſons, their heirs and aſſigns, in fee ſimple or in fee tayle, or for term of life, or lives, or years, to be held of them the ſaid Edward earl of Clarendon, George duke of Albemarle, William earl of Craven, John lord Berkley, Anthony lord Aſhley, Sir George Carteret, Sir John Colleton, and Sir William Berkley, their heirs and aſſigns, by ſuch rents, ſervices and cuſtoms, as ſhall ſeem fit to them the ſaid Edward earl of Clarendon, George duke of Albemarle, William earl of Craven, John lord Berkley, Anthony lord Aſhley, Sir George Carteret, Sir John Colleton, and Sir William Berkley, and their heirs and aſſigns, and not of us, our heirs and ſucceſſors; and to the ſame perſon and perſons, and to all and every of them, we do give and grant by theſe preſents, for us, our heirs and ſucceſſors, licence authority and power, that ſuch perſon or perſons, may have or take the premiſes, or any parcel thereof, of the ſaid Edward earl of Clarendon, George duke of Albemarle, William earl of Craven, John lord Berkley, Anthony lord Aſhley, Sir George Carteret, Sir John Colleton, and Sir William Berkley, their heirs or aſſigns, and the ſame to hold, to themſelves, their heirs or aſſigns, in what eſtate of inheritance ſoever, in fee ſimple or in fee tayle, or otherwiſe, as to them and the ſaid Edward earl of Clarendon, George duke of Albemarle, William earl of Craven, John lord Berkley, Anthony lord Aſhley, Sir George Carteret, Sir John Colleton, and Sir William Berkley, their heirs and aſſigns, ſhall ſeem expedient; the ſtatute in the parliament of Edward, ſon of King Henry, heretofore King of England, our predeceſſor, commonly called the ſtatute of *Quia emptores terrarum*; or any other ſtatute, act, ordinance, uſe, law, cuſtom or any other matter, cauſe or thing heretofore publiſhed

part thereof to him or them that will purchaſe the ſame.

liſhed or provided to the contrary, in any wiſe, notwithſtanding.

The lords proprietors impowered to confer titles of honour.

XIII. And becauſe many perſons born or inhabiting in the ſaid province, for their deſerts and ſervices, may expect and be capable of marks of honour and favour, which, in reſpect of the great diſtance, cannot conveniently be conferred by us; our will and pleaſure therefore is, and we do by theſe preſents give and grant unto the ſaid Edward earl of Clarendon, George duke of Albemarle, William earl of Craven, John lord Berkley, Anthony lord Aſhley, Sir George Carteret, Sir John Colleton, and Sir William Berkley, their heirs and aſſigns, full power and authority, to give and confer, unto and upon, ſuch of the inhabitants of the ſaid province or territory, as they ſhall think do or ſhall merit the ſame, ſuch marks of favour and titles of honour, as they ſhall think fit, ſo as their titles or honours be not the ſame as are enjoyed by, or conferred upon, any of the ſubjects of this our kingdom of England.

And to erect forts, caſtles, cities, towns and other fortifications.

XIV. And further alſo, we do by theſe preſents, for us, our heirs and ſucceſſors, give and grant licence to them the ſaid Edward earl of Clarendon, George duke of Albemarle, William earl of Craven, John lord Berkley, Anthony lord Aſhley, Sir George Carteret, Sir John Colleton, and Sir William Berkley, their heirs and aſſigns, full power, liberty and licence to erect, raiſe and build, within the ſaid province and places aforeſaid, or any part or parts thereof, ſuch, and ſo many forts, fortreſſes, caſtles, cities, burroughs, towns, villages and other fortifications whatſoever, and the ſame, or any of them to fortify and furniſh with ordnance, powder, ſhot, armour and all other weapons, ammunition and habilements of war, both defenſive and offenſive, as ſhall be thought fit and convenient for the ſafety and welfare of the ſaid province and places, or any part thereof, and the ſame, or any of them, from time to time, as occaſion ſhall require, to diſmantle, diſfurniſh, demoliſh and pull down, and alſo to place, conſtitute and appoint, in or over all or any of the ſaid caſtles, forts, fortifications, cities, towns and places aforeſaid, governors, deputy governors, magiſtrates, ſheriffs and other officers, civil and military, as to them ſhall ſeem meet, and to the ſaid cities, burroughs, towns, villages, or any other place or places within the ſaid province or territory, to grant letters or charters of incorporation, with all the liberties, franchiſes and privileges requiſite or uſual, or to, or within this our kingdom of England, granted or belonging;

and

and in the ſame cities, burroughs, towns and other plaecs, to conſtitute, erect and appoint, ſuch, and ſo many markets, marts and fairs, as ſhall in that behalf be thought fit and neceſſary, and further alſo to erect and make in the province or territory aforeſaid, or any part thereof, ſo many mannors with ſuch ſignories, as to them ſhall ſeem meet and convenient, and in every of the ſaid mannors, to have and to hold a court baron, with all things whatſoever which to a court baron do belong, and to have and to hold views of franck pledge and court leet, for the conſervation of the peace, and better government of thoſe parts, with ſuch limits, juriſdictions and precincts, as by the ſaid Edward earl of Clarendon, George duke of Albemarle, William earl of Craven, John lord Berkley, Anthony lord Aſhley, Sir George Carteret, Sir John Colleton, and Sir William Berkley, or their heirs, ſhall be appointed for that purpoſe, with all things whatſoever, which to a court leet or view of frank pledge do belong, the ſaid courts to be holden by ſtewards, to be deputed and authorized by the ſaid Edward earl of Clarendon, George duke of Albemarle, William earl of Craven, John lord Berkley, Anthony lord Aſhley, Sir George Carteret, Sir John Colleton, and Sir William Berkley, or their heirs, by the lords of the mannors and leets for the time being, when the ſame ſhall be erected.

Power to levy, muſter and train men, and make war.

XV. And becauſe that in ſo remote a country, and ſcituate among ſo many barbarous nations, the invaſions as well of ſalvages as other enemies, pirates and robbers, may probably be feared; therefore we have given, and for us our heirs and ſucceſſors, do give power by theſe preſents, unto the ſaid Edward earl of Clarendon, George duke of Albemarle, William earl of Craven, John lord Berkley, Anthony lord Aſhley, Sir George Carteret, Sir John Colleton, and Sir William Berkley, their heirs and aſſigns, by themſelves, or their captains, or other officers, to levy, muſter and train up, all ſorts of men, of what condition,ſoever or whereſoever born, whether in the ſaid province or elſewhere, for the time being; and to make war, and purſue the enemies aforeſaid, as well by ſea as by land, ; yea, even without the limits of the ſaid province, and by God's aſſiſtance, to vanquiſh and take them, and being taken, to put them to death by the law of war, and to ſave them at their pleaſure; and to do all and every other thing, which to the charge and office of a captain general of an army belongeth, or hath accuſtomed to belong, as fully and freely as any captain general of an army hath had the ſame.

And to exercise martial law.

XVI. Alſo, our will and pleaſure is, and by this our charter we give and grant unto the ſaid Edward earl of Clarendon, George duke of Albemarle, William earl of Craven, John lord Berkley, Anthony lord Aſhley, Sir George Carteret, Sir John Colleton, and Sir William Berkley their heirs and aſſigns, full power, liberty, and authority, in caſe of rebellion, tumult or ſedition, (if any ſhould happen) which God forbid, either upon the land within the province aforeſaid, or upon the main ſea, in making a voyage thither, or returning from thence, by him and themſelves, their captains, deputies or officers, to be authorized under his or their ſeals for that purpoſe: to whom alſo, for us, our heirs and ſucceſſors, we do give and grant, by theſe preſents, full power and authority, to exerciſe martial law againſt mutinous and ſeditious perſons of thoſe parts, ſuch as ſhall refuſe to ſubmit themſelves to their government, or ſhall refuſe to ſerve in the wars, or ſhall fly to the enemy, or forſake their colours or enſigns, or be loiterers or ſtragglers, or otherwiſe howſoever offending againſt law, cuſtom or military diſcipline, as freely and in as ample manner and form as any captain general of an army, by virtue of his office, might or hath accuſtomed to uſe the ſame.

The province of Carolina & the inhabitants thereof to be ſubject immediately to the crown of England.

XVII. And our further pleaſure is, and by theſe preſents, for us, our heirs and ſucceſſors, we do grant unto the ſaid Edward earl of Clarendon, George duke of Albemarle, William earl of Craven, John lord Berkley, Anthony lord Aſhley, Sir George Carteret, Sir John Colleton, and Sir William Berkley, their heirs and aſſigns, and to all the tenants and inhabitants of the ſaid province or territory, both preſent and to come, and to every of them, that the ſaid province or territory, and the tenants and inhabitants thereof, ſhall not, from henceforth, be held or reputed a member or part of any colony whatſoever in America, or elſewhere, now tranſported or made, or hereafter to be tranſported or made; nor ſhall be depending on, or ſubject to their government, in any thing, but be abſolutely ſeparated and divided from the ſame: and our pleaſure is, by theſe preſents, that they be ſeparated, and that they be ſubject immediately to our crown of England, as depending thereof for ever; and that the inhabitants of the ſaid province or territory, nor any of them, ſhall at any time hereafter be compelled, or compellable, or be any ways ſubject or liable, to appear or anſwer to any matter, ſuit, cauſe or plaint whatſoever, out of the province or territory aforeſaid, in any other of our iſlands, colonies or dominions in

America,

America, or elſewhere, other than in our realm of England and dominion of Wales.

The lords proprietors impowered to grant liberty of conſtience.

XVIII. And becauſe it may happen, that ſome of the people and inhabitants of the ſaid province, cannot in their private opinions conform to the public exerciſe of religion, according to the liturgy, form and ceremonies of the church of England, or take and ſubſcribe the oaths and articles made and eſtabliſhed in that behalf, and for that the ſame, by reaſon of the remote diſtances of thoſe places, will, as we hope, be no breach of the unity and conformity eſtabliſhed in this nation, our will and pleaſure therefore is, and we do by theſe preſents, for us, our heirs and ſucceſſors, give and grant unto the ſaid Edward earl of Clarendon, George duke of Albemarle, William earl of Craven, John lord Berkley, Anthony lord Aſhley, Sir George Carteret, Sir John Colleton, and Sir William Berkley, their heirs and aſſigns, full and free licence, liberty and authority, by ſuch ways and means as they ſhall think fit, to give and grant unto ſuch perſon and perſons inhabiting and being within the ſaid province or territory, hereby, or by the ſaid recited letters patents, mentioned to be granted as aforeſaid, or any part thereof, ſuch indulgencies and diſpenſations in that behalf, for and during ſuch time and times, and with ſuch limitations and reſtrictions, as they the ſaid Edward earl of Clarendon, George duke of Albemarle, William earl of Craven, John lord Berkley, Anthony lord Aſhley, Sir George Carteret, Sir John Colleton, and Sir William Berkley, their heirs or aſſigns, ſhall in their diſcretion think fit and reaſonable; and that no perſon or perſons, unto whom ſuch liberty ſhall be given, ſhall be any way moleſted, puniſhed, diſquieted, or called in queſtion, for any difference in opinion or practice, in matters of religious concernment, who do not actually diſturb the civil peace of the province, county or colony that they ſhall make their abode in; but all and every ſuch perſon and perſons, may from time to time, and at all times, freely and quietly have and enjoy his or their judgments and conſciences in matters of religion, throughout all the ſaid province or colony, they behaving peaceably, and not uſing this liberty to licentiouſneſs, nor to the civil injury or outward diſturbance of others; any law, ſtatute or clauſe, contained or to be contained, uſage or cuſtoms of our realm of England, to the contraryhereof, in any wiſe notwithſtandng.

XIX. And in caſe it ſhall happen, that any qoudts or queſtions ſhould ariſe, concerning the true ſenſe and un-

In case of doubts or questions, the interpretation to be made most advantageous and favourable to the lords proprietors.

derstanding of any word, clause or sentence, contained in this our present charter, we will, ordain, and command, that at all times, and in all things, such interpretation be made thereof, and allowed in all and every of our courts whatsoever, as lawfully may be adjudged most advantageous and favourable to the said Edward earl of Clarendon, George duke of Albemarle, William earl of Craven, John lord Berkley, Anthony lord Ashley, Sir George Carteret, Sir John Colleton, and Sir William Berkley, their heirs and assigns, although express mention, &c.

Witness ourself at Westminster, the thirtieth day of June, in the seventeenth year of our reign.

Per ipsum Regem.

F I N I S.

This Day are publiſhed,

Debates of the Houſe of Commons of Ireland, during the Years 1763 and 1764. Dedicated, by Permiſſion, to the Earl of Chatham. Taken by Sir James Caldwell, Bart. Two Volumes ——	0	12	0
Proteſts of the Lords of Ireland, from the firſt upon Record ———	0	3	6
All theſe Parliamentary Books being printed in 8vo, *complete Sets* may be had, uniformly bound, gilt and lettered, in Twenty Volumes ———	6	6	0

The REMEMBRANCER; or, Impartial Repoſitory of Public Events. Publiſhed Monthly. Price One Shilling each Number.

Extract from the Plan of this Work.

The intereſting Advices from America, ſuggeſted the Utility of a periodical Collection of the beſt Accounts of every important Public Tranſaction. Many events have happened which probably will be the ſubject of future Diſcuſſion. The Execution of the Work is its beſt Recommendation. It is humbly offered to public Conſideration. In brief, the Plan is, to ſelect from all the public Prints, American and Engliſh, the beſt Account of every material Public Event; to print it in Octavo; and at the End of every Volume to add a copious Index. Three Volumes are already publiſhed. The Work began in June, 1775, at the Commencement of Hoſtilities; and hath been continued Monthly to the preſent Time.

The INTERIOR Country of North America, from Montreal to New-York, which is become the Theatre of War, between the King's Troops and the Americans, is faithfully and accurately delineated in Governor Pownall's Map of the Middle Provinces. In this Map, all the Rivers, Falls, Lakes, Iſlands, Creeks, Towns, Forts, Hills, &c. are to be found, with their reſpective Names; ſo that the Routs of the ſeveral Armies, their occaſional Poſts, &c. may be traced with the greateſt Eaſe and Exactneſs. This Map, having been collated and examined with the Surveys now lying at the Board of Trade, may be depended upon for Authenticity. It is further rendered uſeful, by a curious and copious topographical Deſcription of the Country. Price 10s. 6d.

The new preſent State of GREAT BRITAIN. Containing an Account of the Government of Great Britain; the Power, Prerogatives, and Revenues of the King; the Laws, Cuſtoms, and Privileges of Parliament; and the Power and Methods of Proceeding in the ſeveral Courts of Juſtice. A Deſcription of the Capitals of England and Scotland, their Government, Courts of Juſtice, principal Buildings, Trading, and other Companies, Privileges and Commerce, &c. &c. New Edition. Price 5s. bound.

A COLLECTION of all the Treaties of Peace, Commerce, and Alliance, between Great Britain and other Powers, from the Revolution (in 1688) to the preſent Time. Two Vols. 12s.

Printed for J. ALMON, oppoſite *Burlington-Houſe, Piccadilly.*

www.ingramcontent.com/pod-product-compliance
Lightning Source LLC
Chambersburg PA
CBHW031450270326
41930CB00007B/931
* 9 7 8 3 3 3 7 2 7 4 3 5 1 *